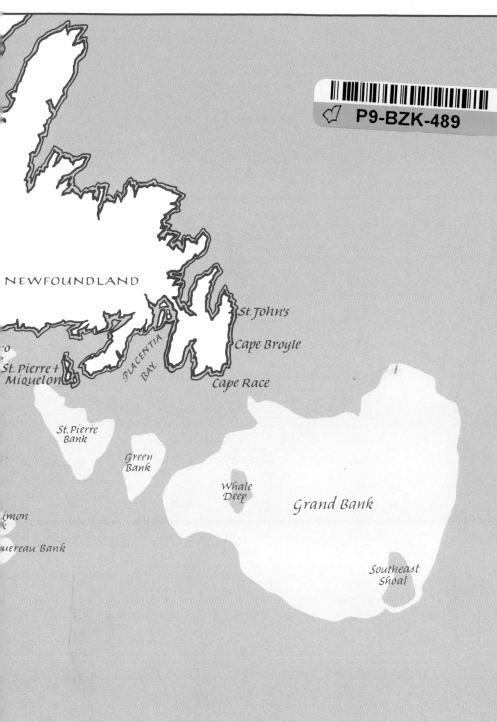

NEWFOUNDLAND

St. John's

Cape Broyle

Flemish Cap

St. Pierre +
Miquelon

PLACENTIA
BAY

Cape Race

St. Pierre
Bank

Green
Bank

Whale
Deep

Grand Bank

imon

uereau Bank

Southeast
Shoal

P9-BZK-489

OTHER BOOKS BY JOSEPH E. GARLAND

Lone Voyager: The Biography of Howard Blackburn

That Great Pattillo: The Biography of James William Pattillo

Eastern Point: A Nautical, Rustical and Social Chronicle of
    Gloucester's Outer Shield and Inner Sanctum 1606–1950

Boston's North Shore: Being an Account of Life among the
    Noteworthy, Fashionable, Wealthy, Eccentric and Ordinary
    1823–1890

DOWN TO THE SEA

The Fishing Schooners of Gloucester

They that go down to the sea in ships, that do business in great waters: These see the works of the Lord, and his wonders in the deep. For he commandeth, and raiseth the stormy wind, which lifteth up the waves thereof. They mount up to the heaven, they go down again to the depths: their soul is melted because of trouble. They reel to and fro, and stagger like a drunken man, and are at their wits' end. Then they cry unto the Lord in their trouble, and he bringeth them out of their distresses. He maketh the storm a calm, so that the waves thereof are still. Then are they glad because they be quiet; so he bringeth them unto their desired haven. *Psalm 107*

DOWN TO THE SEA

The Fishing Schooners of Gloucester

JOSEPH E. GARLAND

David R. Godine, Publisher · *Boston*
in association with
CAPE ANN HISTORICAL ASSOCIATION

First published in 1983 by
David R. Godine, Publisher, Inc.
Post Office Box 450, Jaffrey, New Hampshire, 03452
in association with Cape Ann Historical Association
Gloucester, Massachusetts

Copyright © 1983 by Joseph E. Garland
Introduction copyright © 1983 by Sterling Hayden

All rights reserved. No part of this book may be used or reproduced in
any manner whatsoever without written permission, except in the case
of brief quotations embodied in critical articles or reviews.

Plans for "Lion," "Essex," "Grace Darling," "Onato," "Grace L. Fears,"
and "Puritan," reproduced from *The American Schooners, 1825–1935*,
by Howard I. Chapelle, by permission of W. W. Norton & Company, Inc.
Copyright © 1973 W. W. Norton & Company, Inc.

Library of Congress Cataloging in Publication Data

Garland, Joseph E.
    Down to the Sea.

    Includes index.
      1. Fisheries—Massachusetts—Gloucester—History.
2. Schooners—Massachusetts—Gloucester—History.
3. Ship-building—Massachusetts—Gloucester—History.
4. Fishing boats—Massachusetts—Gloucester—History.
SH222.M4G37   1983   338.3'72709744'5   82-49340
ISBN 1–56792–141–8

Second Edition

Printed in Hong Kong

🌊 *Frontispiece*: The handsome 116-foot Indian Head Gloucesterman *Ingomar*,
designed by Tom McManus and built by Tarr and James at Essex in 1904,
ghosts out of Gloucester Harbor in full dress not long after launching.
(Herman W. Spooner, Thomas Collection)

To

Paul Kenyon
Bill Sibley
Gordon Thomas

Gloucestermen

CONTENTS

INTRODUCTION

Among the endless legends of man's struggle with the sea none is more magnificently moving than that of the fishermen hailing from Gloucester, Massachusetts.

So singular this saga, so steeped in grief and glory, so redolent of old-fashioned Blowed-in-the-Glass Romance (forgive me, Gloucester), that few among us today even begin to comprehend the true meaning of a word long held in something close to sheer awe by generations of seafaring and literate folk the world over: *Gloucestermen.*

But brace yourself and hang on, for help is on the way and lies just up ahead among the pages of this remarkable book from the pen of Joc Garland, a denizen of Eastern Point, a seaswept granitic promontory appended to old Cape Ann as though fashioned for the precise purpose of giving Gloucester the noble harbor we know to this day.

Gloucester gave the world a type of sailing vessel the like of which will never be seen again. She sent down to the eternal sea those schooners that took her name, that in a way were almost the mirror image of that great brawling young giant of a nation known as the *USA.* No chauvinism here. The ships speak for themselves. Take a quick squint at the photographs embedded in this book and you'll begin to comprehend, I trust, what it is I'm driving toward.

From roughly 1870 to 1930 this town, along with her handmaiden Essex, brought to life a wondrous swarm of two-masted, two-fisted, sweet-sheered vessels calculated to do battle with that malevolent wilderness of waters known as the North Atlantic Ocean. Their everyday task was to catch fish, but their niche in maritime history is due in no small part to their incomparable ability to battle to windward in the teeth of living gales. To say nothing of their capacity to heave to and ride out some of the most daunting weather and infuriate conditions to be found rampaging around on the surface of the Seven Seas.

They were also beautiful. Now we're getting down to it. Working craft the world around have usually had sea-keeping qualities. But beauty? Soaring, mind-boggling beauty? Now that is something else. Even Gloucester herself, never given to flights of fancy, had a phrase for her pelagic progeny: *able handsome ladies*. Able was for going to windward, for driving, slashing, slamming uphill full in the face of those infamous winter northwesters, iced up sometimes halfway to the hounds, with their men hard-pressed to endure twenty-minute watches, with pure hell breaking loose aloft and the devil himself dancing a jig downwind, his arms widespread in a welcoming arc for those too weary or weak to survive.

Handsome to Gloucester meant the set of the spars, the flawless proportions, the balance of rig and gear, the planes and curves of handsewn cotton canvas. Small wonder that the mere mention of *Gloucesterman* was enough to command sharp respect and even wonder wherever seafaring men congregated, causing many to indulge in an interlude, however brief, of unabashed reflection.

And is there not some irony in the fact that, for some of us at least, no schooner yacht ever built could measure up for sheer un-varnished beauty to those great tall-sparred, long-boomed, latter-day racing-fishing schooners with that homely word, *Gloucester*, emblazoned round their bulwarks, eight or ten feet aft of the hardbit iron wheel that was every bit as integral to a Gloucesterman as the band of bedbugs playing footsie in the fo'c'sle? Yeah.

Now then. When it comes to the men who made those vessels go — and in the making made Gloucester the redoubtable port we're talking about, here again the author has done his subject proud. Done us all proud in fact. For this is also a book about the human condition (working-stiff division). Commercial fishermen of many lands and many climes have a long tradition of working on shares. None of your "Pull up the ladder, Billy, I'm on board" gospel so dear to the hearts of merchantmen and Navy drones. Hell no. How else could such a vast amount of raw work as goes on in the fisheries ever get done? You wolf some food and scald your gut with some coffee and go on deck and plunge headfirst into the job. Work and work and work some more. Great way to get rich.

But, who knows? Maybe there are "riches" in this convoluted world the arbiters of the Fortune Five Hundred way of life don't know damn-all about. One thing for sure: the fishermen enshrined in these pages knew what it was like to bust their guts and haul their hearts out . . . then maybe hang to the vessel's wheel and ease her as she roared toward home and mother with her rail dragging the water, the salt spray rattling like machine-gun fire off whatever canvas might be drawing her back up under the lee of the land. And then one more bitter passage winding down, leaving the Dayvil dangling on his own particular ropes, the stiffs in the fo'c'sle could lather up, belt back a blast of Black Rum . . . and look themselves right square in the eye.

Joe Garland I salute you. You've told it like it was!

Sterling Hayden

PREFACE

It chanced that just as Gordon Thomas was retiring from his North Shore fish market and preparing to move to New Hampshire in 1979, the new leadership of the Cape Ann Historical Association of Gloucester was reviewing its direction and priorities. Certain discussions were held, and Thomas had the wisdom to sell, and the museum the prescience to buy, his hoard of some thirty-five hundred priceless photographs of Gloucester schooners and waterfront scenes from the days of sail, by far the largest such in existence.

Much good in the world, perhaps most of it, is accomplished by secondary intention. The collector's ham-handed sire, Captain Jeff Thomas, had barred his only offspring from following in the risky business of going down to the sea. The landbound son, to some extent consequentially, devoted his spare hours for the next sixty years to an ongoing search-and-rescue mission in behalf of Gloucester's ghostly fleet of sail. Vindication ten times over: Gordon Thomas, more than any other, has kept alive the spirit of our fishing fathers and waiting mothers here and passed it on.

When Harold Bell, the new president of "The Historical," as we somewhat quaintly call our elegant heirloom, suggested that with its backing I put together a book of commentary on a selection of the more striking photographs from their staggering acquisition, I was intrigued. Much of my own feeling for Gloucester and her vessels, beyond my ancestral and youthful connections, was inspired and educated by Gordon. For my writings I had picked his brain and borrowed his pictures unconscionably over the years. The restoration of old gaff-rigged boats, messing around with them and even sailing them, including a small schooner of thirty-five feet, had given me much pleasure. And I had long harbored the notion that I might one day attempt a history of the Gloucester fisheries that was more flesh and wood than fish and statistics.

The proposition had to be approached warily, however. Most of the field had been preempted. Gordon Thomas had already issued a brace of evocative books, bristling with information about the vessels and the waterfront,

Fast and Able and *Wharf and Fleet.* The final major work of the late naval architect and historian Howard I. Chapelle, *The American Fishing Schooners,* was the biblical authority on their development, design and construction while the ink was still wet. Dana Story, whose sire was the most prolific of the Essex shipwrights, had captured the lore of the building, the men and the methods as no other ever has or can in his engaging classic, *Frame-Up!* And then, going back, there was the unparalleled living record of the fisheries bequeathed by George H. Procter over his forty-odd years as editor of the *Cape Ann Weekly Advertiser,* the powerful first-hand prose of Captain Joseph W. Collins, G. Brown Goode's monumental survey of the industry of a hundred years ago, the graphic fiction of Rudyard Kipling and James B. Connolly, and a whole shelf of contemporary fascination with the mystique of the Gloucestermen.

My tactic, then, was to seize upon Hal Bell's innocent proposal as the pretext for poaching the preserves of my more knowledgeable predecessors and mentors without a qualm but with the heartfelt gratitude that I hereby hasten to acknowledge. My vague aim was to capture and convey through words and images, to the extent that an *ex post facto* nonparticipant can, the *feel* of sailing out of this mysterious harbor when it was a veritable forest of masts.

The most graphically exciting publisher we could think of, David R. Godine of Boston, agreed to join in, and we were under way. But not before I got the feel myself of the heaving deck and mighty sailing power of the last of the working Gloucestermen as the guest of Captain Jim Sharp and his wife, Pat, aboard their ancient schooner *Adventure,* once Captain Jeff Thomas's, windjamming the Maine coast.

J.E.G.

1. THE GLOUCESTERMEN

No important era has passed from the American scene as abruptly as the age of commercial sail. Nor as prematurely, as we are beginning to realize in our current energy-conscious rediscovery of the wind. Let us hope that where movement to and fro over the oceans of the earth is concerned, past may indeed be prologue. The breezes will be always with us.

The packets and the clippers and the merchantmen, the whalers, the bankers, the hookers, jiggers, trawlers and seiners — victims of the diesel engine. The squat coasters and the hulking coal and grain and lumber and salt carriers — done in by World War II. The stone sloops and woodboats and a hundred other subspecies of ocean workhorses — are all gone save for a few surviving square-riggers sentimentally maintained at exorbitant expense for show and seamanship training, the carefully unjammed wind-jammers in the Maine cruise trade, the dwindling fleet of skipjacks still oystering Chesapeake Bay, and the aged hulks eking out their dotage as dockside restaurants and museums.

Of all this ghostly armada, none held on longer or paid off more handsomely at a more horrible cost in lives and living than the Gloucester fishing schooner. No class of vessels in history, possibly, served its home port in so paradoxical a role as both servant and master. The men and the schooners of Gloucester, in the days when she sent forth more of both to bring back more fish than any other port in the world, were in the eyes of the world as one. *Gloucestermen* they were called with wonder, schooners and men, so close was the symbiosis — some might say the deadly embrace — of town and sea.

The schooners of Gloucester were never, contrary to traditional nautical genderizing, notably feminine. Over the two and a quarter centuries of their evolution they sailed in all shapes and sizes, keeping in common only the characteristic rig of the type. Yet they were a breed apart, the product of Yankee pragmatism, reflecting the demands, sometimes the fads, and too often the tragic misconceptions of the day.

Rough and tough and dirty were the Gloucester schooners. Regular stomach-turners, fast or slow, rollers or pitchers, seaworthy or sea-wary,

1

workhorses, racehorses or plugs, blessed or jinxed, but never *pretty*. The old *Henry W. Longfellow* did not pirouette over a sparkling sea. Fair-weather sailers they were not. Never *ladies* for all the suspicion of yachtiness in the last of them — or almost never, and thank God for the exceptions.

Almost always these distinctive vessels, which could invariably be identified by the way their very proximity dilated the nostrils and quickened the pulse, were *Gloucestermen*, whether named for the women who waved from the wharf and waited, or for the owners who peered out on the harbor from the security of their waterfront offices and skimmed off the profits or shook off the losses.

Romance of the sea and distant shores? None, unless you didn't have to go fishing for a living. Rudyard Kipling was "immortally seasick" while getting the feel of it for *Captains Courageous*. Only James B. Connolly, the runner-up champion of the yarn-spinners, had the stomach for the offshore stuff. Artists captured their oft-painted subjects from safe on terra firma. Few photographers outside of Albert Cook Church relished the dubious ambience of dirty socks drying by the galley stove. Rare indeed the Gloucesterman, the ubiquity of the Kodak notwithstanding, who saw enough unusual about doing business on great waters to bother packing a camera with his duds.

If not romance, was it something else akin: a fatal flirtation? a death wish? a life wish? Some soulful force that drives or draws men to see for themselves the works of the Lord, and His wonders in the deep?

Some years back someone reached for a figure, and it was commonly stated, as if in good Gospel round numbers, that ten thousand men of Gloucester had gone down to the sea forever. The mortality for the first two centuries is in fact not recorded. But the record does state with certainty that during the sixty-eight years between 1830 and 1897, an absolute minimum of 668 Gloucester schooners and 3755 Gloucester men sailed out and never sailed back.

In 1879 alone Gloucester lost twenty-nine schooners — very nearly one tenth of her entire tonnage — and 249 fishermen. Thirteen vessels and 143 men went to the bottom of Georges Bank in a single gale on the night of February 20. That was the most devastating of a string of bad years, and the worst storm, in the recorded history of the North Atlantic fisheries.

The harbor from which schooners by the thousands upon thousands and men in the hundreds of thousands have gone fishing for 360 years is a huge indent in the south coast of Cape Ann, as rockbound a sentinel of Massachusetts Bay to the north as Cape Cod is sandy to the south. Twenty-five miles to the northeast of Boston, the port of Gloucester is among the largest and securest on the coast and the closest to the major fishing banks of the North Atlantic. The outer bay — the greater harbor — is a mile wide, two miles long, open to the southwest but fairly protected from the full smash of

2

the sea and the northeast storms by the great peninsula of Eastern Point, though only since 1905 by the Eastern Point breakwater as well.

The French explorer Samuel de Champlain discovered the expansive, luminous beauty of Gloucester Harbor in 1606 and named it "Le Beauport." In 1623 a couple of shiploads of English fishermen-adventurers set up a fishing stage on the mainland shore of the harbor. But the sea was as cruel as it was prolific, and the wilderness pressed at their backs. This first settlement of the Massachusetts Bay Colony was abandoned after two or three almost unbearable winters, and the first fishermen backed off to a less harsh shore, where they founded Salem.

By 1640 Gloucester had been resettled and incorporated. The first cod-fishery in the New World had been reestablished. Some houses, wharves and the fish-drying frames called flakes clustered at the head of Harbor Cove, far inside the secure inner harbor, itself a cul de sac buffered from the sometimes seething outer harbor behind Ten and Five Pound Islands and the sheep pasture of Rocky Neck.

At about the same time a second fishery sprang up in the village of Annisquam, where the tidal Annisquam River empties and fills on Ipswich Bay, which buffets the north coast of Cape Ann in a northeaster. Other Gloucester fishing outposts clung to the exposed beaches east of 'Squam at Hodgkins Cove, Plum Cove, Lane's Cove, Folly Cove, and, on the bold ocean shore, Pigeon Cove and Sandy Bay. But all were mere teacups alongside Gloucester Harbor.

Marblehead rivaled Cape Ann for several generations as America's chief fishing port, mainly through the tenacity of her fishermen, for her much smaller harbor faces opposite Gloucester's, right into the teeth of the north-east storms. Like Salem and Newburyport, Marblehead suffered irreparably from the Embargo and the War of 1812. There is no doubt, too, that at some point about 150 years ago circumstances came together, fate anointed Gloucester, natural superiority of situation prevailed, and its growth accel-erated at the expense of the numerous other fishing stations from southern New England and Cape Cod to the coast of Maine and beyond.

Yet the 'Headers hung on and continued to dominate the distant and dangerous Grand Bank codfishery of Newfoundland to which they early had adapted their own version of the schooner, the "heeltapper," so called because its quarterdeck, raised to give the men safer freeboard while fish-ing in rough weather, made it look like an upside-down boot. In 1837 Marblehead fitted out 122 codfishing vessels of all sizes, comparing remark-ably with the 221 Gloucester sent forth in the cod and mackerel fisheries. The smaller port rode the crest of its wave as a force in the fisheries in 1839, boasting ninety-five schooners over fifty tons.

Seven years later disaster knocked Marblehead out of the business as a force forever. A tremendous, suddenly shifting gale swept the Grand Bank

3

on September 19, 1846, taking eleven schooners and sixty-five men and boys. Absolutely numbed, the town next year fitted out only fifteen schooners, and never recovered from the loss. Gloucester had long since achieved domination of the industry when an 1851 census credited the harbor with 241 schooners in the mackerel fishery alone, followed by Wellfleet on Cape Cod with seventy-nine.

Gloucester's ascendancy in the American, and during her zenith the world, fisheries persisted through virtually the whole era of sail up to the outbreak of World War II. The story of the heyday of American fishing in the Western Ocean is the story of fishing under sail, the bittersweet saga of the Gloucestermen.

Few colonial vessels outlasted their day, no plans or proper models of one — such a dearth as to provoke Gloucester's chief historian, John J. Babson, to lament 120 years ago that "our information is hardly sufficient even to enable the imagination to represent satisfactorily their form and appearance when under sail."

The first sailing craft were of necessity familiar types brought over from Britain or built here, shallops and ketches mostly. The shallop was a double-ended boat propelled by oars or by either a fore-and-aft, sprit-rigged mainsail or by a two-masted setup with square sails. Being undecked, the shallop was suitable only for the inshore fishery.

The larger and more versatile ketch was commonly employed on the offshore banks and was the forerunner of the schooner, in the opinion of the late naval architectural historian William A. Baker. The colonial ketch carried two masts, the larger mainmast forward, the shorter mizzen aft. Though combinations of rig varied greatly, Baker thought that the ketch was generally larger than the shallop, with round stern, flush deck, frequently setting a lateen mizzen sail and sprit mainsail, sometimes a main-topsail.

Of the lore today is the oft-repeated account of Andrew Robinson's supposed "invention" of the schooner at Gloucester in 1713, given credence and some *ex post facto* documentation by Babson in his 1860 *History of the Town of Gloucester*. Modern students of the evolution of ship design are still arguing the matter, the more skeptical school tending to dismiss this "event" as apocryphal chauvinism. Nevertheless, it is probably true, as Babson related, that around 1713 Captain Andrew Robinson, a mariner of great standing in the community, built a fishing vessel on the east shore of the harbor's Smith Cove, just south of what is today Reed's Wharf, that he rigged in an unusual but unrecorded style.

At the launching the unusual vessel slid into the cove so smoothly as to inspire a spectator to exclaim, "Oh, how she scoons!" (to skip a flat stone on the water, according to Babson's etymology), at which her delighted builder is supposed to have declared: "A scooner let her be!" Thus Robinson

4

christened his new craft, and unintentionally a new type. How the *h* got in there is another mystery.

That is John Babson's story, based on accounts written by Dr. Moses Prince in 1721 and Cotton Tufts in 1790. Another version, ferreted out from the *Gloucester Telegraph* of June 1, 1839, has escaped the academics and is amusing enough, appearing as it did twenty-one years before Babson's:

"The first *schooner* ever launched, is said to have been built at Cape Ann in 1714. Her name is not known."

The above item is found in Cooper's late work on the Naval History of the United States. The manner in which this description of vessels received the appellation, "Schooner," is not a little curious. We were quite young at the time [sic!] but recollect that as the craft glided into her element, an old lady among the spectators exclaimed in the fullness of her gratification — "La me, see how beautifully she *scoons!*" "Beautifully, beautifully," responded all the men, women and children assembled. "Then," said her owner, "let her be called 'Sc(h)ooner,'" and in the twinkling of an eye the old black bottle of Jamaica was dashed against her prow in confirmation of the christening!

Not a mention of Andrew Robinson in the *Telegraph* editor's little yarn, nor a word about skipping stones.

In the exhaustively studied opinion of one modern authority, E. P. Morris, "the plain fact is that the Gloucester tradition leaves us exactly where we should be if the story had never been recorded." In *The Fore-and-Aft Rig in America* Morris scoffs at Babson's earnest effort to document Gloucester's traditional claim to invention of the rig it immortalized as without substance technically. That joyful outburst, "Oh, how she scoons!" Morris suggests, was "made up in an attempt, perhaps a humorous attempt, to account for the word "scooner.'" Alas, they will not let us have our innocent traditions.

Be all this as it may, *schooner* was rapidly taken up along the coast in the first quarter of the eighteenth century and applied, as most of the experts of modern times seem to agree, not to a particular hull form (as it never has been) fashioned by Captain Robinson, but to a new wrinkle in rig.

Morris found evidence of a rudimentary schooner-type rig in an English print of about 1700. Baker wondered if the Robinson version might have involved his adaptation of the even older and presumably familiar Dutch rig, possibly via New York, to the New England ketch: that is, the mizzen-mast gives way to the mainmast, which is moved ahead of the cabin trunk and abaft the now shorter foremast — the characteristic spar layout of the schooner. Babson also guessed that Robinson may have been the first in these parts to hang "trapeziform" sails, stretched out at the foot by booms, from wooden gaffs.

Everyone has had at it. Merritt Edson in *The American Neptune* magazine theorized that the word *schooner* was first applied locally by Robinson to the familiar small fore-and-aft colonial coasters of his time, rigged with a foreyard and squaresail, then to a modified fishing ketch by 1720, and in the 1740s to designate both versions of the rig.

The great yachting editor Thomas Fleming Day proposed in a 1906 issue of his *Rudder* magazine that perhaps Robinson rerigged what Day interpreted as a "brigantine" employed in the bank fishery, pushing the after mast forward and hoisting a fore-and-aft sail. The name might be a corruption, he mused, of the Norman-French *escumer*, a skimmer, a fast vessel.

That Andrew Robinson lived, and where and when, is certain, and that he lived an extraordinary, adventurous and quite well-documented life, even serving as Gloucester's representative to the General Court in Boston. Although, unhappily, he left behind no record of his unusual invention, adaptation or whatever it was, and the real nature of that first schooner remains a question mark, it is a fact that within five or six years more and more New England fishing and coasting vessels were being called "schooners," and ever since Gloucester has been as closely identified with the type as coal is with Newcastle.

Why did the schooner catch on so quickly with the notoriously conservative fishermen? Because it was demonstrably faster than the ketch, probably. Schooners fly more canvas than ketches, and under most conditions sail faster under a more balanced and versatile sail plan, especially with fishermen doubling as crew.

It may also have been a pleasant surprise for those first schoonermen to discover that their vessels could jog along on the banks, under foresail only, barely creeping ahead a trifle off the wind, perhaps with the jib held to windward as well, and that in a gale of wind they could lie to with some minimum of ease under double-reefed mainsail alone.

The knack of the schooner for beating to windward and crawling off a lee shore is probably as much a factor of hull as of rig. Still, if the colonial ketch was antiquated by its successor as rapidly as it would seem, the superior weatherly ability of the new rig can be almost taken for granted. A long thrash to weather on one leg or another of a fishing trip — home against the prevailing southwesterly in summer, out against an easterly or fighting the winter nor'wester deep-laden on return — were all in the day's work, season in, season out. For a large fishing or merchant vessel working the North Atlantic coast with and against the alongshore breezes, no higher pointing arrangement than the schooner's has been devised. And off the wind, don't they crack off the knots!

An inherent disadvantage to windward in the old schooners was Babson's "trapeziform" sail. The gaff rig developed as a supposed improvement over the lateen as a means of spreading more fore-and-aft sail. Wire rigging, turnbuckles and new masting techniques introduced the yachtsmen's much more windwardly triangular Marconi sail. Gaff-riggers go great guns when presenting all that spread of sail a little off a good steady breeze, though they can be mighty dangerous in a squall. But although you can sheet in the main and fore booms of a fishing schooner when beating (and the fore gaff via a special sheet called a vang back to the mainmast, rarely bothered with), the all-important main gaff persists in sagging off to lee-ward, carelessly spilling much of the big sail's forward drive. Gaff topsails and the fisherman's staysail slung between the masts helped to windward, but only when the breeze was moderate enough to carry them. An occasional Gloucesterman, by some quirk of design or sail or rig or handling, seemed to perform wondrously on the wind, comparatively speaking. But there is just so much you can get out of a gaff-rigged vessel when it comes to pointing. The schooner slugged along against (rarely into) the teeth of it well enough to stay out of trouble — or to get out of it — most of the time.

One who knew whereof he spoke on this score was the curmudgeonly naval architect L. Francis Herreshoff of Marblehead, who unburdened himself in his *The Common Sense of Yacht Design* of a few disdainful observations concerning the breed:

Generally speaking, a vessel without much stability that cannot be driven hard to windward will be easy on her hull. This is the condition with fishing vessels, and their hulls are often surprisingly weak; some of them are a pile of unseasoned lumber with a few trunnels driven haphazardly, but they hold together, for it is impossible to drive them hard to windward. Their weight is too high up to allow them to carry sail in a breeze. Surely Gloucester fishing schooners have been driven hard on a reach or running free, but it is beyond the realm of possibility for a fishing schooner or a fisherman-construction yacht to be driven hard close hauled.

To which this author, once the master of a Nova Scotia-built gaff-rigged schooner yacht of thirty-five feet, can but whisper amen.

For their first hundred years or so the New England fishing schooners were bluff of bow, broad of beam and high of stern. The Marblehead heeltappers slid off the ways at up to seventy-five tons gross, sixty feet long on deck. When not fishing (and the winter's first surge of Arctic air descended from Canada with the nor'wester), some skippers were apt to make a run down to the West Indies to see what could be bartered for a cargo of salt fish and lumber, carrying along a brace of squaresails to take advantage of the beckoning trade winds. The reputation of the bankers for speed, relatively, and of the sailor-fishermen for their seamanship and knowledge of the coast recommended the crude colonial schooners for service in the nascent American Navy and as privateers during the Revolution.

7

Almost nonexistent are the artifacts and sketchy the evidence surviving even into the early nineteenth century. Fortunately, the late Howard I. Chapelle, naval architect of note and the leading authority on the development of American sail, reconstructed in some cases and literally saved in scores of others the lines and plans of archetypal schooners and small sailing craft in general that, but for his energetic and intuitive research, would have been lost forever. His last book, *The American Fishing Schooners: 1825–1935,* will probably remain the definitive work on the subject.

Along with the high-pooped heeltappers, as Chapelle notes, at least two other distinct schooner types had emerged by the eve of the War of 1812. One was a smaller fishing craft being spawned in awesome quantities on the banks of the Chebacco River where it was and is bridged by the road between Gloucester and Ipswich. This community, built around family shipyards, was Ipswich's south parish, called by the Indian name of Chebacco, which in 1819 was incorporated as the town of Essex. These "Chebacco boats" rarely exceeded thirty tons and forty feet and might qualify as primitive schooners, for the foremast was stepped way up in the "eyes," practically in the stem, catboatwise, and they carried neither bowsprit nor jib, only a pair of gaffheaded sails. Some were double-enders; others, with square sterns, were known as "dogbodies" — and dogs they look to the modern eye.

Fleets of Chebacco boats sailed out of the various harbors and coves of Cape Ann in the inshore fisheries, so successfully that by 1792, Babson reported, 133 of them "resorted to the ledges and shoal grounds near the coast, where they found, at different seasons, cod, hake, and pollock; and pursued their fishery with such success, that, in twelve years . . . the number of boats engaged in it had increased to about two hundred, while the tonnage had nearly doubled."

With the resumption of commerce and the westward expansion of the frontier, fish was in high demand after the War of 1812. But the American fisherman never has had much political clout, and the peace commissioners at the Convention of 1818 bargained away his historic free access to Canadian waters and accepted a ban on fishing within three miles of the coast of the Maritime Provinces that excluded most of the bays where the mysterious mackerel had, by 1830, put in their cyclical reappearance in biblical numbers. "The fishermen follow the fish, not the law," as even today they are wont to say, and three miles be damned. And so the Yanks must have bigger and faster schooners, able to track the schooling mackerel east to the Bay of St. Lawrence and beyond, fast enough to run for home, with a deckful of poached mackerel, leaving astern, perchance, Her Majesty's revenue cutters.

Enter the immortal "pinky" with its kittiwake-tail stern raised as pertly as a pinky finger, surviving as a fisherman right into the early twentieth century, thriving today in certain out-of-the-way anchorages as an atavistic schooner yacht in the hands of appreciative traditionalists.

Narrower and sharper than the heeltappers, with a deeper grip on the water and no doubt faster, the pinkies were keen on the windward haul and much superior as mackerel chasers and cutter flee-ers. Their more cramped cabins, however, and the rocking-horse sterns that kept them happily cantering in a seaway, also kept them out of the mainstream of schooner design, the more to the liking of their old-fashioned adherents who hung on to a dwindling few of the stoutly built Methuselahs and nursed these ghosts of a long bygone era from the twilight of colonial times into the dawn of the air age.

Three pinkies first tried fishing for cod on the tricky shoals of Georges Bank, 125 miles to the southeast of Gloucester, in 1821. They anchored and were so whipped around by the rip tides that nine years passed before Captain John Fletcher Wonson of East Gloucester and his crew screwed up the courage to tackle the Georges again. They found the great bank teeming with gigantic halibut, discovered they could anchor and fish without being dragged under by the current after all, and thus opened up the richest fishery in the North Atlantic.

There followed a resurgence of shipbuilding and a wave of enthusiasm for the well smack, a schooner with fish hold sealed off fore and aft by water-tight bulkheads, a kind of floating aquarium that communicated with the ocean outside through numerous holes bored in the planking. The aim was to keep the catch, even halibut, alive on the trip home and fresh for market. Not wholly foolproof, as one might suspect.

On the fishing grounds 150 years ago the old methods persisted. Once arrived, the schooner anchored or jogged under shortened sail, the crew at the rails trying to avoid tangling their lines while they plied the bottom for the deep dwellers — the cod, haddock, hake and pollock — and the groundfish — old halibut and sole. Or, with men in the mastheads on the lookout, they searched the sea for the shimmering school of mackerel which, once found, was tolled, or enticed, to the surface alongside with a noxious slick of ground-up bait known as "chum." Then the men crowded the rail, flinging over their handlines armed with long hooks, the shanks of which were encased in lead, "jigs." Jigged, hooked or whatever, the fare, large and small, was cleaned and salted right on deck and, when the hold was full, carried back to Gloucester, or to Boston if the price was better, for resalting, drying, packing and shipping.

The old methods persisted, and so did the old notions of design. The vessels were a bad lot — crude, shallow, top-heavy, slow, dull to windward and dangerously prone to knockdown. "While all of these were practical objections to the type," Chapelle wrote ironically, "none of them were really valid reasons for discarding the old model, for the safety of fishermen

9

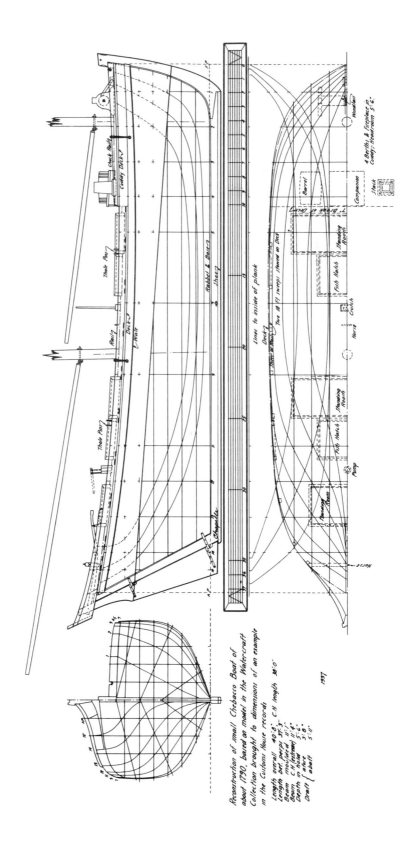

Lion, Chebacco boat, 1804

DOWN TO THE SEA

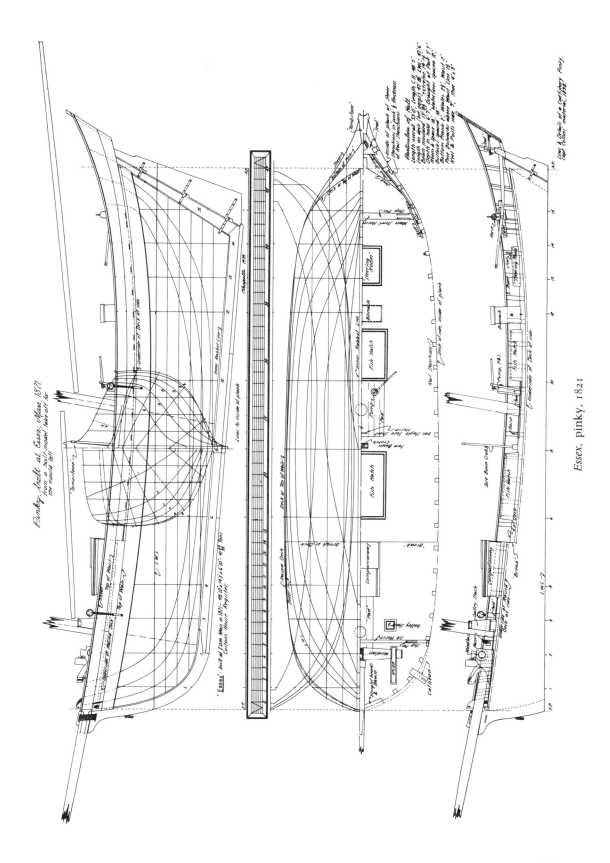

Essex, pinky, 1821

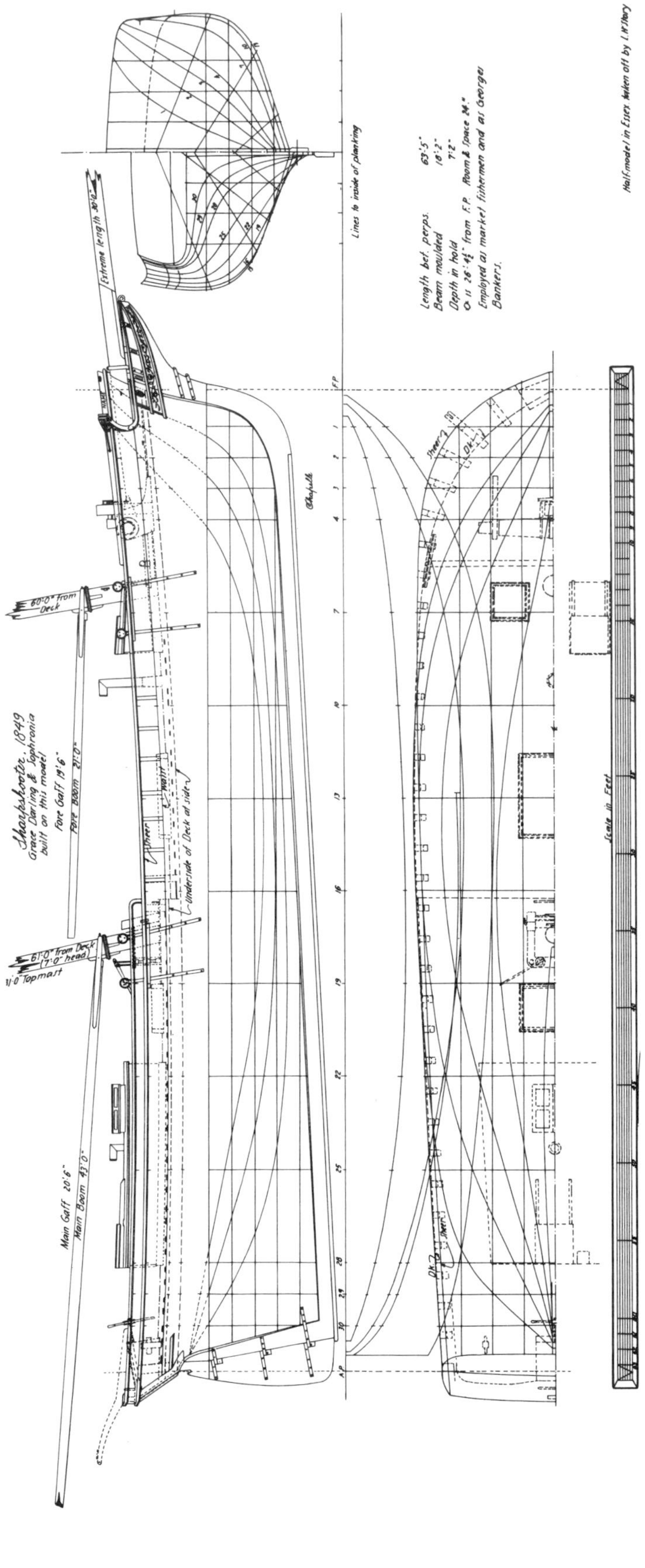

Lines to inside of planking

Length bet. perps.   63'5".
Beam moulded   18'2".
Depth in hold   7'2".
○ " 28'-4½" from F.P. Room & Space 14".
Employed as market fishermen and as Georges
Bankers.

Half-model in Essex taken off by I.N'Ilbury

Sharpshooter, 1849
Grace Darling & Sophronia
built on this model

Fore Gaff 14'6"
Fore Boom 28'0"

Extreme length 70'0½

Main Gaff 20'6"
Main Boom 43'0"

Underside of Deck at side

60'0" from Deck

61'0" from Deck
(7'-0" head)
1/ 0 Topmast

Scale in Feet

Grace Darling and Sophronia, sharpshooters, 1849–1850

Baiting trawls on board the Gloucester haddock schooner *Mystic*, about 1883 (Goode's *Fisheries*)

13

and vessel property were not always prime considerations in the improvement of vessels, the brutal facts being that the men lost cost the shipowner nothing, and insurance could take care of the loss of vessel property."

Vessel insurance may not have been quite the blanket that Chapelle represents it to be, but lost lives were indeed no more than a matter of regret to the owners, and his wry comment as to their motivation applied almost as aptly to the evolution of schooner design for the next fifty years.

So it was not conscience that inspired a new look at design, but the almighty dollar. By early in the 1840s ice was being cut from the ponds of Cape Ann in the winter and packed in sawdust in icehouses for year-round distribution. Chopped ice replaced the live well overnight in the market schooners, and ever so much more satisfactorily. Chopped ice at one end, and the extension of the railroad from Boston to Gloucester in 1847 at the other, between them put a new premium on speed: the first boat in to Gloucester (or Boston's T Wharf) with a well-iced fare of fresh halibut, haddock or mackerel was the harbinger of the fleet and won the top dollar from the dealers in the bidding. Furthermore, there can be little doubt that the tragic loss of the cream of Marblehead's fleet in the gale of 1846 was Gloucester's gain.

Out of the competitive ferment of those watershed 1840s emerged a true departure in fishing-schooner design. They called them "sharpshooters," long of hull and straight of keel, almost flat on the bottom, sharp bilges, and graced with the first suspicion of that slightly hollow, racy, slicing bow that would be the immortal mark of the clipper ships. The sharpshooters were at first eyed with suspicion by the old-timers on the Gloucester waterfront, who predicted that any vessel deprived of a good bluff bow would nose under and drown herself if anchored on the tide-ripped shoals of the Georges.

In reality, as fair-weather sailers the sharpshooters proved beamy enough to stand up to more canvas than any of their predecessors, faster than anything ever seen out of Gloucester, and sufficiently shoal of draft to continue berthing in the shallow, mostly undredged and frequently undredgeable docks of the inner harbor. Nor did they nose-dive on Georges Bank. As foul-weather sailers, the sharpshooters were probably no worse than their sires. In the sharpshooter, the Gloucester schooner achieved its identity.

Not only as fishermen had the schooners proved themselves by the middle of the nineteenth century. They were the odd-jobbers of the coast, lugging anything that could be loaded aboard from anywhere to anywhere, or nowhere — the cove or harbor too remote to be freighted in or out of by land. Small, smart schooners, none faster or more seaworthy, were raced out by the pilots to meet incoming vessels requiring local knowledge to thread in through Boston Harbor. Gloucester fishermen and other gold-

14

struck forty-niners from nearby ports organized mining companies, bought fishing schooners and pounded around the Horn to California to find out for themselves if anything was in them thar hills. Transplanted, the schooner took hold on the West Coast as a fisherman and carry-all.

Nor was it all fishy bilges and the appetizing aroma of salt horse and black beans drifting around deck from the galley stack. Crêpes Suzette, caviar and cognac found their way aboard too. Custom-built schooner yachts with professional skipper and paid hands had been the playthings of Boston China traders for many years when the first regatta east of Cape Cod was sailed off Nahant in July 1845 by eleven shining yachts, every one a schooner. Six years later the New York Yacht Club's rake-sticked schooner *America* brought home the Royal Yacht Squadron's Hundred Guineas Cup, never yet returned. Schooners dominated for another thirty years and are to this day the ultimate objects of yearning for yachtsmen imbued with sentiment and a sense of maritime history and the fitness of things.

One may wonder how in the world the saltwater country hamlet of Essex found the room for fifteen shipyards on the mudbanks of its tidal creek, or how they built and launched 170 fishing schooners in one three-year stretch of the 1850s. Or where Gloucester a generation before its peak found the dockage, let alone the swinging room in the anchorage, for a fishing fleet that long before the Civil War was growing at an astonishing rate. In 1828 that fleet was comprised of 154 vessels over twenty tons (most of them, if not all, schooners), as well as some square-riggers in the foreign trade and numerous sloops and smaller craft in the inshore fisheries. In sixteen years, by 1844, the number had increased to 189. By 1859 the fleet stood at 301 schooners crewed by 3568 men and boys, augmented by another fleet of smaller craft. Together they brought in, that year alone, 60,000 barrels of mackerel, 11,400,000 pounds of codfish and 4,590,000 pounds of halibut, and a few million more of haddock, hake, pollock, herring, sole and other species, lobsters and clams, tongues, sounds and oil.

The Civil War interrupted a traditional trade — a look-the-other-way trade in cheap salt fish with the plantation owners of the South — and was not universally popular in Gloucester, where some skippers were not above the thrilling challenge of circumventing the Union blockade. Likewise, the town had since the end of the Revolution enjoyed a practical monopoly of trade with Surinam, or Dutch Guiana, on the South American coast, where salt fish — slave fodder — was bartered for rum, sugar, fruit, spices and fine wares from Holland. Already fading with the rise of abolitionism, this lucrative traffic was given the coup de grace by the Dutch when they banned slavery in the colony in 1863. Not a proud chapter in Gloucester's history.

With peace, fishing and shipbuilding were vigorously resumed. Regular steamship service between Boston and Gloucester opened up a whole new

15

channel for fisheries products. And two of the four technological revolutions to overcome the conservative industry (the third and fourth were the otter trawl and the quick-freezing process) practically overnight catapulted Gloucester into the mass-production business and raised the town (incorporated as a city in 1873) to its dominant position as the leading fishing port in the world.

The first of these great innovations was the perfection of the purse seine with which in one swoop the mackerel fishermen, if lucky, were enabled to net an entire school or the better part of it within a matter of minutes. What a contrast to the old way, one by one and two by two over the rail! By the early 1870s jigging was hardly more than a way of killing time.

The second postbellum piscatorial revolution involved the widespread adoption of dory-trawling, a pursuit that *ipso facto* was not as innovative as its multiple application to the ingenious, and all too frequently in its consequences awful, conception of the schooner as mother ship. Now one man, instead of fishing with four hooks at a time, could fish with four hundred — and at only ten times the risk to himself.

Like so many changes profound in their implications, dory-trawling was profoundly simple. Formerly a dozen or so crew lined the rail, tending a brace of handlines each, hoping for the wily codfish or the hungry halibut to convene for dinner twenty fathoms below the vessel's bottom.

Dory-trawling changed all that, except on Georges Bank, where the tides were too strong for small craft and miles of bottom gear, and handlining persisted. Off dory-trawling, the Gloucester schooner of the late 1860s and the 1870s now carried six or eight of these double-ended, flat-bottomed, rowing-sailing skiffs nested on deck. Once on the grounds, the schooner anchored and put over the dories with their tubs of trawl. Two men to a dory, they would fan out, bending to the oars to a likely spot, maybe a mile or more from the vessel. Over splashed a barrel buoy, and at the end of the buoy line an anchor to which was tied the beginning of a mile, say, of fishing line, the trawl, paid out of the trawl tub. And from that trawl were strung the short, light ganging (ganjin') lines, thousands of them, each ending in a baited hook. At the end of the trawl, over the side with another anchor and buoy.

Trawls set, the dories rowed back to the schooner for the coffee breaks traditionally known as mug-up. Rowed out again and underran the trawls until each pair of dorymates had hauled a ton or so of codfish or halibut aboard. Back to the schooner, pitch 'em up over the rail on deck, and up most of the night cleaning and salting down a fare that would have taken the handliners a week or two to catch.

Dory-trawling was an all-season, all-weather, day-and-night pursuit, bitterly cold, fog, snow, squall, gale, blizzard, collision, freezing spray, frostbite, capsize, lost, drown or starve to death.

16

As the fortunes of Gloucester rose with the tide of world demand, dealers and processors and packers, owners and skippers, bankers and builders pushed and pushed for the high line, for the top stock, for the fastest vessel, the most reckless crew, forever haranguing for speed, for that press of sail. "Drive her, boys, drive her!" Jim Connolly loved to have his thinly fictionalized captains roar into the teeth of the gale — out to the banks and fish and home, night and day, fair weather and foul, first in to market for that top dollar, and first back out.

The sharpshooters, in this first wave of the mania for speed, grew sharper and longer and flatter on the bottom and more seductively clipperlike. Vast mainsails, huge mainbooms hanging away off astern, kites of topsails, jib upon jib shivering back from outthrust bowsprits that dipped into every green sea to sweep a man from the footropes, the "widowmakers."

Surprisingly rapidly, and with a seeming disregard for the lives of the men who must sail them, the owners and designers turned from the old sharpshooters and embraced the new clippers in their obsession with speed. Many factors, certainly, contributed to the staggering losses following the Civil War, when in the twenty-five years between 1866 and 1890 Gloucester lost 382 schooners and 2454 fishermen. All of these men didn't go down with their ships, nor did every ship let down its men. Dories capsized or went adrift. Men were washed overboard, fell out of the rigging, or were struck by booms. Schooners were lost through negligence or in storms and under conditions that no vessel could be expected to survive. All the same, as Chapelle has been quoted on an earlier generation of schooners, " . . . the men lost cost the shipowner nothing, and insurance could take care of the loss of vessel property."

And finally, when the carnage was at its worst a hundred years ago, did the stoic fishermen and the widows and the orphans of the victims rise up in their wrathful sorrow and demand an end to it? No, they were voiceless. Nor did the union, for there was none. Nor the owners, who cared not. Nor the government, which knew not.

It was a master mariner who had been through it and seen it all and had survived to have some influence in fishing circles and in Washington, a compassionate newspaper editor, and a few others of their stripe who denounced the old ways and spoke up for reform.

Captain Joseph W. Collins was a self-educated Gloucester skipper, one of the best and most fearless of his day, who had been through hell in a long career at sea. His expert knowledge of all aspects of the fisheries raised him to a highly respected position with the United States Commission of Fish and Fisheries in Washington. Appalled by the crescendo of losses, and an articulate and powerful writer, Captain Collins mounted a personal campaign for greater safety in the New England fisheries through design reform. He immediately drew the support of George H. Procter, editor of the *Cape*

17

Ann Weekly Advertiser, and then of other influential figures concerned with the fisheries.

The payoff came in 1885 with the launching of the commission's plumb-stem research schooner *Grampus*, the inspiration of Collins, the creation mainly of Dennison J. Lawlor, East Boston designer and builder. *Grampus* broke the mold of blind habit and inertia. It was as if the veil had been lifted. One might think the designers had rediscovered the wheel, in this case the first principle of the seaworthy sailing vessel known by every boy who ever whittled out a model with a jackknife: depth of hold and low center of gravity, according to which, if one adheres to common sense, the more she tips, the more she wants to right herself. They had but to look around them at the last surviving pinkies, reproachful reminders of forgotten basics, and ask themselves, How?

Grampus and a few other pioneers led to the big schooners of the turn of the century, the knockabouts, the "Indian Headers," the powerful wine-glass hulls with deep keels and yachty lines, and finally to the breathtakers of the 1920s and 1930s, lofted to race the fastest of the Canadians and to fish enough to qualify — the be-all and end-all of the Gloucestermen in their magnificent dying days.

How ironic that a pure-bred schooner should at last be achieved even as the breed was fading out! As ironic, in a way, as the surrender of Congress, finally, to forty years of lobbying for a massive granite breakwater just as the need to shelter a fleet of fishing schooners in the outer harbor of Gloucester was obscured in a cloud of diesel smoke.

And then the third revolution: steam power, diesel power and the adoption of the otter trawl, the dragnet no sailing vessel could haul effectively across the bottom of the sea, wind or no wind, scooping in every creature in its path. And the disappearance, as if by the wave of a wand, of the subsociety of sail — the skills, the wisdom, the vessels, tools, support systems, customs, traditions and even language. A culture wiped out forever.

The balance of power between man and fish, between predator and prey, had for centuries been moderated — sometimes this way, sometimes that — by wind and wave. With the interjection of machinery and technology into the equation, the scales have tipped, perhaps decisively. Wind power and sails, hooks and lines, even seines — too chancy, too slow, too arduous, too patient, too *balanced*. Or were they?

1

1. The crew of a Chebacco boat, the primitive fishing schooner of the post-Revolutionary period, drails, or trolls, for mackerel while under way off the Cape Ann shore. Masts are short, sturdy and unstayed. Note mooring bitt in bow and the typical pink stern of the vessel broad on in the distance at left. (Goode's *Fisheries*)

2. A "heeltapper" of the 1830s period lies at anchor on the Grand Bank, crew at the rail handlining for cod. The high poop deck evidently was intended, like the "apple bow," to brush off boarding seas. (Goode's *Fisheries*)

2

1

2

20

3

1. The pink-stern schooner *Senator*, built at Essex in 1831, fishes for pollock on the "Old Southeast" bank near Halfway Rock off Marblehead, the only pinky out of Gloucester when the photograph was taken in 1883. Anchored aft of this well-preserved antique is a small lapstraked two-masted fishing and lobster boat, probably rigged with spritsails. (U.S. Fish and Fisheries Commission, courtesy of Al Barnes and The Mariners' Museum)

2. Captain Rufus Smith at the wheel of the pinky *Maine*, built at Essex in 1845, at Gloucester in 1910. The drum of the wheel is supported by the heavy horse beam running athwartships and moves the tiller with ropes. The crotch in the sloping "tombstone" sternpiece supports the boom when the mainsail is furled. The tiller opening in the deck doubles as a "head." (Albert Cook Church, courtesy of Charles Sayle and The Whaling Museum)

3. Part of the Gloucester fleet rides at anchor in the inner harbor, probably early 1870s, looking from Rocky Neck. (Thomas Collection)

4. The sharpshooter *Racer*, built at Essex in 1852, jogs off Pavilion Beach in Gloucester's outer harbor in 1882, waiting for the rest of the crew to come aboard. She carries the single big "jumbo" jib common to the earlier schooners. It is fitted with a short boom, a "club," to help the sail set to best advantage, and a "bonnet," the horizontal seam of which can be made out; this is a separate cloth laced to the foot of the jib that can be detached in order to shorten sail when it comes on to blow. The breezy Pavilion Hotel, on the site of the modern Tavern, was among the pioneer summer hostelries on the North Shore of Boston. The spire belongs to the First Universalist Church in America, erected in 1805. Crewman Thomas Kirby was lost overboard from the *Racer* when she collided with the schooner *Electric Flash* in April 1878. (U.S. Fish and Fisheries Commission, courtesy of Al Barnes and The Mariners' Museum)

4

1. The wind is about dead ahead from the southwest as an unidentified banker hitches a short tow out of the crowded inner harbor in 1882. Abreast of Ten Pound Island, with room to tack, the line will be cast off. The schooner directly in line with the towers of Gloucester City Hall is the new *Nellie N. Rowe.* Half hidden behind the vessel under way is the *Edward E. Webster*; beyond, at a Duncan's Point wharf, a salt barque already well lightened; and over their bowsprits the Baptist Church steeple. Alfred Meyers was lost overboard from the *Webster* on the Grand Bank of Newfoundland on July 4, 1876 (overcelebrating the Centennial?), and Edward Coles and Howard Powers drowned from their dory the following April. The year after, Willis Bateman was lost overboard when the *Webster* collided with the *Hereward* on the banks in May 1878. (U.S. Fish and Fisheries Commission, courtesy of The Smithsonian Institution)

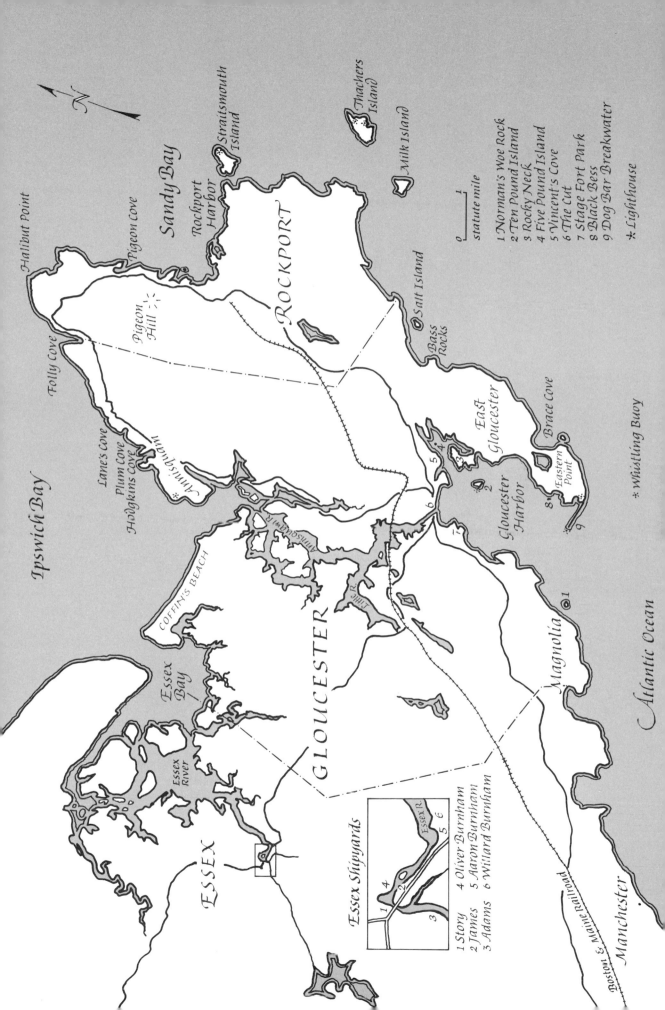

Ipswich Bay

Halibut Point

Folly Cove

Lane's Cove
Plum Cove
Hodgkins Cove

Pigeon Cove

Sandy Bay

Rockport Harbor
Straitsmouth Island

Thachers Island

Milk Island

ROCKPORT

Pigeon Hill

Annisquam

ESSEX

Essex Bay

Essex River

Coffins Beach

GLOUCESTER

ANNISQUAM R.

LITTLE R.

Salt Island

Bass Rocks

East Gloucester

Gloucester Harbor

Brace Cove

Eastern Point

Magnolia

Manchester

Boston & Maine Railroad

Atlantic Ocean

* whistling buoy

N

0   1
statute mile

1 Norman's Woe Rock
2 Ten Pound Island
3 Rocky Neck
4 Five Pound Island
5 Vincent's Cove
6 The Cut
7 Stage Fort Park
8 Black Bess
9 Dog Bar Breakwater

* Lighthouse

Essex Shipyards

1 Story   4 Oliver Burnham
2 James   5 Aaron Burnham
3 Adams   6 Willard Burnham

Essex R.

1

1. In the spring of 1921 Arthur D. Story explains a half-model to Essex youngsters, with one of his finished products in the background, the *L.A. Dunton*, now restored at Mystic Seaport in Connecticut. The traditional first step in the design of a Gloucesterman, long before anyone thought of drawing lines on paper, was the whittling of a lift half-model of the hull. The wooden "lifts," held together by dowels, could be separated to represent the shape of the hull at various horizontal sections, simplifying the reproduction of the full-sized lines in the moulding loft. (Dana A. Story Collection)

2. Thomas F. McManus of Boston and Arthur D. Story were at the height of their fame as designer and builder of fishing schooners when the two paused for the camera at the Story yard in Essex, probably early 1920s. (Walter McNaney Collection)

3. The last of the master loftsmen at Essex, Archer B. Poland, lines off another vessel on his loft floor. When finished, his moulds in vertical cross section will be taken to the yard and laid out on the rough-cut oak, which will be sawed and hewn and pieced to the exact dimensions of each frame. (Story Collection)

2

3

1. Some of the gang at the Arthur D. Story yard in Essex. A.D. knew every phase of the building intimately, though his son Dana testifies that he had no carpentering ability himself. The sixty men in his yard in 1901 turned out eighteen vessels, mostly schooners but including a towboat and a small steamer, averaging 108 tons, all by hand except with the aid of one steam-powered band saw and a trunnel lathe. At one time that spring A.D. had nine vessels on the ways. (Story Collection)

2. "Frame-up!" is the cry that musters the shipyard gang to raise another pair of ribs along the backbone keel of the elongating skeleton at the Story yard in Essex. (E.J. Story, Story Collection)

3

3. Schooner in frames at John Bishop's yard on Vincent's Cove, Gloucester inner harbor, probably 1890s. Frames are held in place temporarily by battens as the planking proceeds up from the keel, starting with the garboards. A "dubber" works ahead of the plankers, dubbing or fairing off high spots on the frames with his adz so that the next plank will snug to every one. A fast team of plankers could fit and fasten two strakes, or rows of planks, a day, both sides, including steaming the wood for the hard twists. The white oak or yellow pine planking was hand-ripped two or three inches thick by two men working a pit saw, one up and one in the pit, before the first steam band saws arrived in Essex in the 1880s.

Brothers John and Hugh Bishop, from Miramachi, New Brunswick, were building fishing schooners and smaller craft in Gloucester as early as 1872. John launched about 150 schooners between 1881 and his death in 1912, most of them from the yard on Vincent's Cove he took over from David Alfred Story, where he had been foreman, when Story retired in 1890. An active scene of fish wharves, shipyards and other waterfront industry, Vincent's Cove was largely encroached upon and filled in by World War I and is memorialized today by a vast cold storage warehouse, busy Rogers Street and parking lots. (The Smithsonian Institution, courtesy of Peabody Museum of Salem)

1. The formidable heft of the Gloucesterman is evident in one of a series of photographs by Albert Cook Church of a schooner under construction at John Bishop's yard around 1909. The gent in the derby hat, boring at the rate of a penny a hole, could make as much as five dollars a day. His mate pounds in the locust trunnels that anchor the outside planking and the interior ceiling on which they're working to the immense oaken frames that have been doubled to span the long and artfully designed curve from keel to rail. The trunnels swell to wed wood to wood, and unlike iron fastenings, they don't rust. (Alfred Cook Church, The Whaling Museum)

2. The large knockabout schooner *Knickerbocker*, 159 tons, nears completion at the A.D. Story yard at Essex in 1912. The caulkers are almost done with the deck. The chisel-like caulking iron and heavy hollow mallet, with a ringing percussion sweet to the ears of the shipwright, lie on deck at left. Cotton and oakum have been pounded into the V-shaped seams, which will be paid (sealed) with hot pitch. The graceful camber of the deck shrugs off water through the rail scuppers, and the planks are about two inches thick — wider, thicker planking forms the mainmast and foremast beds and the broad "strongback" running between them. The portion of the main cabin above deck is the trunk, planked about as thick as the deck. The knots in the white pine sides have been spotted with shellac to keep the pitch from bleeding through the white paint when it is applied. Behind the break in the deck is the great beam, the heaviest athwartships member in the vessel at the point of greatest strain, just ahead of the mainmast. The break also raises headroom amidships. Galvanized iron chainplates with *lignum vitae* deadeyes lie to the right, ready for bolting through the outside planking and the appropriate frame; they take the whole strain of the weather shrouds from the masts when under sail. (Story Collection)

3. At Willard A. Burnham's, somewhat north of the opposite end of the Essex causeway from the yards of Story and Tarr and James, a trim clipper schooner takes shape around 1890. The top or sheer planks just below the rail will be applied after the main and fore chainplates have been bolted through the exposed upper ends of the frames called stanchions, a method abandoned about this time in favor of fastening them to the outside of the hull. The workman under the pole bowsprit appears to be boring for a fastening through the decoratively carved billethead. (Figureheads were never fancied on the workaday schooners of Gloucester.) His companion just abaft the bowsprit shroud spreader is fitting the hawse hole, through which the anchor cable runs, for the cast iron outboard hawse pipe flange that lies on the staging at his feet. Nothing shows off the lines of a schooner as when she is naked of paint. The outboard joiners have done planing the hull, all by hand, first lengthwise, then "traversing" crosswise to fair the subtlest of curves so that nary a rise nor dip can be detected. When his co-worker fell sick early on in the planing of *Stiletto* at John Bishop's in 1910, so the family story goes, George Sibley of Rocky Neck finished the job himself, all 105 feet of her. (The Smithsonian Institution)

3

1

🦢 *1.* As round and smooth as the derby of the carpenter eying the camera, a new schooner awaits launching in Tom Irving's yard at Vincent's Cove, 1880s. The waterline has been struck, and the prime coat of paint applied. Irving built fine models, too. (The Smithsonian Institution)

🦢 *2.* On the west shore of the entrance to Vincent's Cove at Gloucester, the clipper halibuter *Grace L. Fears* gets the finishing touches at the yard of David Alfred Story, later John Bishop's until he shifted farther into the cove on the south shore. The bowsprit has been hoisted into place by a tackle from the shears. Chainplates are on, and planking will soon be done. She'll be launched on July 2, 1874. The entrance from the inner harbor to the right is a mere ninety feet wide. Across the way, Joe Call's spar shop; Friend's lumber wharf on the left; out of sight to the left, the Cape Ann Anchor Works at its original location. In nine years Howard Blackburn and Tom Welch will go astray from the *Grace L. Fears* fishing off Newfoundland in a January blizzard. (Thomas Collection)

🦢 *3.* Albeit commonplace, launchings were occasions for great excitement in Gloucester, proceeding as they did down the bosom of the waterfront at Vincent's Cove. Captain Solomon Jacobs's 117-foot *Helen Miller Gould*, designed by Mel McClain and the first large Gloucester schooner to carry an auxiliary engine, careens into the cove from John Bishop's yard on March 29, 1900 before a very large crowd. Preparatory to launching, a cradle was built under the new vessel on the previously greased ground ways, or tracks, to which the cradle's sliding ways were temporarily secured. The hull's supporting blocks were gingerly removed, allowing its weight to come gradually onto the cradle. At the moment of launch two pairs of men simultaneously sawed through the sliding ways up ahead of the bow, and let 'er rip! To prevent the *Gould* from crashing into the wharf opposite (a not unknown occurrence), a new hawser, caught up in two places by weaker lines to break the sudden strain when she fetched up, was led to a heavy anchor sunk in the earth ashore. It worked. The light ropes parted, and she bid up in time against the hawser, though almost uprooting the anchor. (Ernest L. Blatchford, Thomas Collection)

2

3

4

1. SPLASH! Tom Irving's shipyard was directly across Vincent's Cove from Bishop's, immediately east of what is today the rear of the North Shore Theatre, with an equally short run of water in which to fetch her up. Here the small schooner *Actor*, fifty-four feet, built for Captain Jerome McDonald, taildives in on a wintry day in 1902. Checking lines already are coming taut from the bow. (Thomas Collection)

2. The *Bay State* was the sister schooner of the *Knickerbocker*, designed by Tom McManus and likewise equipped with an early crude oil engine. She, too, was started in 1912 but by John Bishop in Gloucester and finished by Owen Lantz, who took over the yard when Bishop's health failed. Lantz told Gordon Thomas years later that on launching day, October 26, "the checking lines held and the *Bay State* came to a stop within three feet of a building on the opposite shore of the cove. He [Lantz] said that the roof of this shed was crowded with people, and when they saw the *Bay State* heading straight for them, he never saw folks scatter so fast." (Thomas Collection)

3. Most Essex launchings created not much more stir than *Mary*'s, sliding so smoothly into the river on her port bilge from Story's yard on March 19, 1912. *Mary* was the last of some fifteen elegant schooners built at Essex to the designs of Arthur Binney, successor to the great Edward Burgess in 1891. Essex in fact favored the side launching by which the new schooner, instead of being let down on an elaborate and expensive cradle, was simply eased over first until her bilge almost rested on one way, the other way under the keel. When the great moment arrived, the men split out the supporting blocks one by one. As the greased way took the full weight of the bilge, she creaked, groaned, started — and in she slid — if everything went right. Now and then it didn't, of course, and she wouldn't budge, and then there was hell to pay coaxing the infant into the water. (Story Collection)

4. All flags flying, the *Henry Ford* — all 139 feet from stem to stern — zooms in a crescendo of spray down Story's ways on April 11, 1922. No pure fisherman, the *Ford*; wealthy Gloucester yachtsmen and the builder himself had an interest in Tom McManus's latest — and the trophy. (Robert W. Phelps, Thomas Collection)

🐦 *1.* The hawsers come taut and the long and twisty tow down the Essex River toward fit-out is under way. The small schooner *Nokomis*, a McClain design of only sixty feet, has just been launched from the Tarr and James yard next the causeway. It is March 12, 1903. Two more schooners are on the ways, one nearly planked, the other only partly framed. No doubt to even things up, sometimes the partners advertised themselves as Tarr and James, sometimes James and Tarr. A few years later *Nokomis* was lost with all hands in a sudden summer gale. (Thomas Collection)

🐦 *2.* Towing around from Essex was an excursion to be remembered. The stack of the tugboat can just be seen dead ahead. The newly launched fishermen were taken the outside route — around Cape Ann where it could get sloppy — to Gloucester Harbor for fitting-out. Smaller vessels, depending on the tides, were occasionally towed the tricky short cut winding amongst the sandbars and flats of the tidal Annisquam River, around the sharp turn under the railroad drawbridge and through the treacherous rips of Blynman Canal, "The Cut," opening under a second drawbridge into the harbor. (Story Collection)

2. THE BUILDERS

Gloucester used up Gloucestermen faster than it could grow and build them. The men it replaced with local wharf rats as soon as they were big enough to pull an oar and bait a hook, and when the town ran short of natives it filled their ranks with imports from seafaring nations on both sides of the Atlantic to a point where, in the 1890s, so they claimed, most of the skippers in the fleet were Bluenoses from the Canadian Maritimes, Newfies and Portagees from the Azores, with an Irishman and a Swede or two thrown in.

For new schooners, needed in the worst and best years by the scores, Gloucester turned mostly to the shipyards of neighboring Essex. Where and how this otherwise bucolic country village of rolling field and billowy marsh, six winding miles of tidal creek from the sea, produced as if from a bottomless well the manpower and skills to build and launch more than four thousand vessels from its muddy banks over a span of three hundred years or so remains a logistic and possibly genetic wonderment.

Why Essex? A simple matter, one might suppose, to put together wooden ships on the shores of such a harbor as Gloucester's, the biggest in Massachusetts next to Boston, with a West Parish on the mainland side of the Annisquam River that even today has a wild look to it, so thick are the stands of timber amongst the rocks and rills. That there was "good timber for shipping" on Cape Ann is a matter of colonial record, and a "very sufficient builder," the excellent English shipwright William Stevens, who was launching vessels into Gloucester Harbor at least as early as 1643.

Yet, though Gloucester never wholly lost the building touch, she remained a consumer of schooners on a profligate scale, only very incidentally a producer. A gazetteer of 1874 reported that the then new city had 2162 dwelling houses and a fleet of four hundred vessels, most of them fishing schooners. Not a mention of shipyards, though there were in fact a couple on the banks of Vincent's Cove, up in the inner harbor, and one or two in Annisquam and East Gloucester. Essex was credited with 316 houses, nary a vessel, and ten shipyards. Whether of flesh or wood, Gloucester could not meet the demand for Gloucestermen.

Down to the edge of those miles of placid salt marsh that buffered Chebacco Parish from the Atlantic grew the virgin timber, and by 1656 the settlers had built a sawmill at the Chebacco River falls a mile above their first shipyards. Although this mere creek took six miles to meander through the marsh to Ipswich Bay, it was launchable and navigable at high tide and not much use for anything else at low except clamming.

Here was an ideal locale for turning out the Chebacco boats so popular with the shore fishermen of Cape Ann just a short sail down the Bay, and that's what one of the first Burnhams did sometime in the first part of the seventeenth century — in his garret, of all places, the story goes, requiring a wall to be torn down to get her out. Thus the Burnhams, the Storys, the Jameses and other ship-carpentering families were on the scene almost from the day of settlement and had settled on shipbuilding from the start. As early as 1668 the parent town of Ipswich set aside an acre on the river at Chebacco Village for the purpose of shipbuilding, the very location today of the most famous, productive and long-lived of them all, and the last, the Story yard.

Harborless, with an ostensibly unlimited supply of raw timber at its back, a sawmill up the stream, and a tight-knit settlement of shipwrights drawn there for the purpose, Chebacco, later Essex, almost from the beginning assumed the function of builder for Gloucester, where the lumber was harder to get back across that barrier of the Annisquam River, where waterfront footage was wanted so much more for the berthing of vessels than for the building of them, and where fishing, fishing for the Sacred Cod, was literally the livelihood of the colony in 1623, and the fishermen its backbone.

The ten shipyards of Essex in 1874 employed only 150 men and were capitalized in the aggregate at $40,000, a pittance. But they produced in that year alone twenty-two schooners, including a brace of three-masters of 519 and 531 tons, a third of 151 and a barkentine of 570 tons.

Herein lies one secret behind the Essex phenomenon: the family yards of the Burnhams and Storys (twenty-four Burnhams and nineteen Storys since the first records in 1815 and Lord knows how many before that), the Jameses, and Moses Adams (as great a launcher in his way as his biblical namesake) and a few others. An archeological fathom deep in wood chips and sawdust, the Essex yards stood side by side above the tide (and a few at one time as far as a mile inland, dragging the boats to the river), two or three ways, a small and weathered shop, enough room aroundabout for lumber storage, and a faithful horse or ox to haul timbers to and fro — a piddling investment even in 1874 of, on the average, $4000 — somewhat less than the cost of a new vessel.

Those 150 workers that year produced around 3270 tons of handmade wooden ships. That's pushing twenty-two tons a man, hardly a candle to Aaron Burnham's a quarter of a century earlier launching twenty-two in twenty-two months.

All by hand. Not until 1884 did Moses Adams break down and bring in the first steam-powered band saw, and the competition was mighty slow to follow suit with such newfangled contraptions. Fifteen men to a yard? No, and herein lies the other secret of Essex's Helenic output. "A remarkable system of building had come about, one which even by present standards must have been extraordinarily efficient." So writes Dana Story, proprietor of the Story yard and fifth in the line, in his authoritative history of it all, *Frame-Up!*, adding, "The secret of all this, I think, lay in the fact that most of the men were specialists in some particular phase of the work."

The craftsmen provided their own tools and, as Story explains, specialized, working individually or in gangs that frequently shifted around from yard to yard according to the stages of progress on the various ways. This division of labor made possible a kind of "mass" production (several schooners were frequently built from identical plans) based not on assembly lines but on assembly gangs. In this way the tiny town of Essex could slip into its remote creek an outrageous number of ships every year, year in and year out, as the end products of a high degree of informal organization and dovetailing of skills.

The Essex phenomenon was a triumph of Yankee community effort, interfamily organization and discipline remarkably akin to the spirit that motivated and governed the men who sailed the schooners.

No question but what shipbuilding in Essex was a shoestring operation. Dana Story claims few made any real money at it. For all his schooner-a-month for twenty-two months, Aaron Burnham went broke. Story's father, the great Arthur D., built 425 vessels between 1873 and 1932 (and sired ten children, Dana the last — by his second wife — when he was 65); but he didn't turn a profit until the final fifteen years of his long career.

Often as not, the Essex builder wound up with a part interest in his product for his pains; fishing was a risky business, and too many owners couldn't or wouldn't pay up. Fortunate the builder who managed to get more than a decent wage out of it. Of course the men weren't paid in full until the boss was. "In full" meant around two dollars a day for a ten-hour day a hundred years ago, six days a week — and lucky to get the work.

The men struck for a nine-hour day and got it, then struck again around 1910 for eight, first in Gloucester, then in Essex, and got it but could never get shut of the sixth day. A committee waited on old John Bishop in Gloucester that time, as Story relates, and informed him they'd decided they were going to work eight hours and that was that. "That so?" said he. "Well, I'm damn glad to hear it."

The staying power of little Essex probably had something to do with the length of the cuff on which her builders were willing or forced by circumstances to put their vessels, the brevity of their capitalization and the informality of their arrangements. Bargaining with the best known of the Gloucester Portuguese skippers out in the yard one day, A. D. Story consummated the deal by picking up a scrap of wood and scrawling on it with his pencil stub: "I agree to build and Captain Joe Mesquita agrees to pay for a vessel of about 65 tons." A handshake would have been good enough for Captain Joe, who read the sea like a book but couldn't write his name.

When it came to financing, there was a working relationship of long duration between the Essex builders, the Gloucester banks and the owners in the hands of many of whom, as time went by, capital and fleets accumulated, owners of honored names such as Rogers, Pearce, Sargent, Wonson, Babson, Garland, Smith, Cunningham and Thompson, Leighton, Jordan, Walen, Chisholm, Mansfield, Steele, Tarr, Parsons, Pew and Gorton.

The very limitations imposed by the depth and breadth of the Essex River on the size of the vessels that could be launched and got out kept the ambitions of the town's builders within good Yankee reason. Plenty of Gloucestermen over the generations came off the ways down East, up the Merrimac River as far as Haverhill and at East Boston, where, for example, the trim clipper fisherman *Joseph Garland*, 51.44 tons old measurement, named for my physician great-grandfather, splashed into Boston Harbor from the yard of Epes Davis, Jr., in May 1866.

But the East Boston and Newburyport builders were really geared to turning out those breathtaking square-rigged clippers in the style of the great Donald McKay, and the enormous multimasted, slab-sided schooners for the coal and lumber trade. Robert K. Cheney notes in his valuable *Maritime History of the Merrimac* that as far back as 1865 the Newburyport men were complaining that fisherman-type schooner and boat construction had declined alarmingly ever since 1815; by the end of the century shipbuilding had about ceased on the river, owing chiefly to a dead low tide in financial backing. Modest little Essex had long since secured a practical monopoly on the fishermen's business, while iron, steam and the vagaries of world commerce did in the wooden dinosaurs.

That the Merrimac shipwrights — one of them at any rate — had the old knack is attested in Cheney's account of the famous Eben Manson, who continued modeling the magic of his speedy schooners long after he retired from active building, whittling out three such for Gloucester owners over a span of six weeks in 1882. "Apparently the Gloucester skippers were tired of looking at the name and scroll work on the sterns of Manson's fishing schooners as they sailed past in charge of Newburyport masters, and coming to the reluctant conclusion that Manson could and did build the fastest fishermen and coasters afloat, decided to have some of the same." So much for Newburyport chauvinism.

38

Such friendly rivalries aside, the fact is that for a hundred years and more Essex bore the major responsibility for replenishing and expanding the biggest fishing fleet in the world with serviceable vessels, delivered when needed at affordable prices. There is no doubt that for a long time the product was as crude as the owners were willing to pay for and the fishermen to put up with. Witness Albert Cook Church's photographs of the ancient pinky *Maine,* typical of the workboats of her day.

And then events began to converge during that germinal period around 1850. The Essex men (and everyone else) woke up to the fact that the local timber was running out just as the new railroads were reaching in to the more remote forests of New England and the West, vying with the lumber coasters plying their trade from the Maritimes to the Carolinas. The rails stretched to new markets too; ice came into general use for refrigeration, the competition sharpened and faster schooners were demanded.

Essex responded with the sharpshooters, which meant finer lines, lighter and more challenging construction. Production soared. From the mid-nineteenth century on, the usually skeptical schooner historian Howard Chapelle judged admiringly, "The quality of construction at Essex was highly praised . . . The vessels were almost yacht-like in finish . . . The men were very jealous of their reputations for quality workmanship. This not only gave quality control but also lightened the load of builders' supervision, allowing one-man control of a shipyard."

Chapelle's praise is at odds with Francis Herreshoff's disdain, already referred to, for the fisherman construction — "Hulls often surprisingly weak; some of them are a pile of unseasoned lumber with a few trunnels driven haphazard." Surely true; there were vessels and vessels, builders and builders. Captain Nat Herreshoff's son capped that derogation, however, with sweeping contempt: "I fear there is almost nothing to be learned from fisherman-construction unless it is how to build a boat that will rot out quickly or fall apart when she strikes terra firma."

Herreshoff enjoyed his choler and was good at it; he may have had a run-in with a builder the previous day when he penned that indictment, or no more than a bad pork chop for lunch. He knew better than most that compared with the sleek beauties his renowned father, the Wizard of Bristol, ushered out of his Rhode Island yard for the millionaires of the New York Yacht Club, the Gloucestermen charging down the Essex ways to fetch up with a thud against the mud bank opposite were of extra heavy and relatively crude construction, rapidly built though not hurriedly, with a close eye to economy and to a life expectancy immeasurably foreshortened by the cruelty of the beating imposed upon them by their calling.

Magician of Marblehead that he was, L. Francis was aware as well of the creations of Herreshoff rivals such as Edward and Starling Burgess, Bowdoin B. Crowninshield, Tom McManus and Dennison Lawlor — and of such master rule-of-thumb modelers as Cape Ann's Tom Irving and Mel

McClain — working fishing schooners of truly yachtlike beauty and construction to match.

Witness the quarters of the new eighty-three-foot mackereler *William H. Jordan*, just brought around from A.D. Story's to Gloucester in May of 1884 and fitted to the taste of her owner-master James L. Anderson, as described in the *Cape Ann Advertiser*: "The cabin is furnished in bird's eye maple and cherry, with black walnut trimmings, white wood panels in drawers and berths. The captain's stateroom with sycamore, bird's eye maple and cherry. The floor is of black walnut and maple. The forecastle is furnished in black walnut and maple and has nine berths and all the conveniences, including closets, lockers, etc. . . . Her cabin is to be furnished in good style, with easy chairs, sofa, etc. . . ." Total cost, ready for sea: $10,000.

Suffice it to say that the stunning yachts that sailed from the drawing boards of the Herreshoffs, crafted as they were with the care of a harpsichord maker, would have made hard weather of it after a few winter trips to the Georges with a few million aggregate pounds of salt codfish reeking in the hold, and L. Francis — for all his entertaining hyperbole — darn well knew it!

So here's to the builders of the Gloucestermen — the Burnhams and Storys and Jameses and Tarrs, Adams and Oxner, McKenzie, Lantz, Poland, Woodbury, Fenton, Cooney, Irving and the Bishops, Doyle, Perkins, Andrews, Sibley, Wetmore and the rest — and old Andrew Robinson. All gone, or their tools laid down. Now the heritage resides in the youthful hands of Bradford Story, son of Dana, keeping the family tradition alive and aloft on the old ground unto the sixth generation with one fine sailing yacht after another that would have warmed the cockles of L. Francis himself, and certainly the sturdy heart of his grandfather.

For Arthur D. Story was seventy-five when in 1930 he launched the last fishing schooner ever to sail out of Gloucester, the white-winged racer *Gertrude L. Thebaud*. Two years later, fifty years ago, Mr. Story laid the last keel of his life, and with it the tradition of the Gloucestermen, to rest forever.

3. FITTING OUT TIME

Having "towed around the Cape" from Essex, in past the Eastern Point Light and Ten Pound Island to the inner harbor of Gloucester and the welcoming wharf of her owner, that spanking new schooner is sparred, ballasted, rigged and canvased under a swarm of workmen, for everyone having to do with this latest addition to the fleet — none more so than rival factions — is on pins and needles to see how she'll perform.

In a matter of days from launching, if all goes well, comes the long-awaited trial trip — and pray for some wind, not too much, just a nice breeze to get her agoin' and through her paces. All connected — wives, a scattering of kids, sweethearts — flock aboard in their Sunday best, crowding the freshly caulked and payed decks from rail to rail until the Old Man wonders how in the world the boys will ever raise sail or find the sheets.

Trial trips of a few hours outside the Point, particularly of highly touted vessels launched in the smiling seasons of the year, were gala affairs requiring perhaps a "collation" spread under a tarp stretched from the main boom back in the harbor, to the strains of the Gloucester Cornet Band and just the right amount of spirituous accompaniment for a town that yearned to be dry but was destined to be forever wet. Invariably the newcomer was pronounced a rival to the fastest in the fleet, a real flyer given any kind of a breeze (if she were trimmed just a mite more by the head), and she'll be a highliner for sure.

A top moneymaker in one fishery, however, was not necessarily high line in all. Some vessels in some fisheries paid for themselves in a year. Others were unaccountably dogs if not downright Jonahs, hoodoos. Some were mackerel killers but couldn't seem to touch a haddock, and vice versa. It depended on who modeled her and who put her together, whether for speed or stability, year-round fishing or Sunday sailing, who her skipper was and who her crew, what kind of grub and what kind of bait, and as much as anything and maybe more, on plain luck.

As Gloucester approached its zenith in the early 1880s, fishing under sail had achieved a sophistication which, except for some further advances in

41

hull design, was not to be materially improved upon in the fifty years that remained to the age of the schooners. The various fisheries were well defined and highly organized, by species, by grounds, by season of pursuit, by methods, by men, and to some degree by vessels.

From seventy-four of the city's eighty-nine wharves 353 schooners in 1882 fitted out at one season or another (some all year round) for the five major North Atlantic fisheries, besides several lesser ones, that were the hunting grounds of the Gloucestermen. That was quite a fleet, and it would be bigger. Lined up tip of bowsprit to end of mainboom, it would have extended close to eight miles, not counting fifty-nine sizable boats, four large fishing sloops, six steamers and Henry Hovey's big schooner-yacht *Phantom*.

The acknowledged lions of the fleet — men and boats — were the fresh halibuters, forty of them in the peak halibut year of 1879 (the catch declined steadily after that and never recovered from fifty years of overfishing), when they landed 8,300,000 pounds of this giant of the flounders. Every month of the year the strongest and fastest of the Gloucestermen dory-trawled the world's deepest fishery — Grand Bank, Banquereau, Green, St. Peter's, Western (Sable Island) and La Have chiefly, anchoring down to 375 fathoms, fishing on occasion almost twice as deep. Furthermore, the enormous catch of the halibuters that year of 1879 was augmented by another three million pounds landed incidentally during the winter by the Georges Bank codfishermen.

For years the Georgesmen were the first, after the halibuters, to venture forth from the snug harbor where they had been laid up from November to February — laid up because no insurance company would cover them during the worst of the winter if they fished. The odds were that bad. Then in the 1870s, when the storm losses on Georges Bank were so absolutely staggering, the owners formed an all-season mutual insurance company of their own. The resulting surge of competition pushed most of the "Georgies" — vessels as good as the halibuters but smaller, averaging about sixty tons — into year-round fishing, getting under way sometimes by January 15 in order to be on the grounds when the first schools of spawning codfish struck in, early in February. In 1880 there were 107 Georgesmen on the bank exclusively, fifty-seven more for part of the season. They made 1430 trips and landed 27 million pounds of cod and 1,125,000 of fresh halibut, all over the rail on the handline.

The Georgesmen and the fresh halibuters had the worst of the cold behind them but the equinoctial gales of March still to suffer through as the bank dory-trawlers and the mackerelers stuck their bowsprits out of hibernation. The vessels of James Mansfield and Sons sailed from Harbor Cove with such regularity late every April that they were known as the Dandelion Fleet. Off for the southern purse-seining, the regulars were joined by

42

winter-weary halibuters, Georgesmen and haddockers looking for respite. Clearing Eastern Point in the windy days of early spring, this great Gloucester mackerel fleet (113 schooners in 1879) was reinforced by kindred mackerel hunters from up and down the coast, all bound for the Chesapeake and Delaware bays where the schools without number would unpredictably make their appearance, just where and from whence no one knew.

The clever purse seine with which a clever and lucky skipper might encircle and entrap the unluckiest part of a school of mackerel — or lose a clever school, every one — had been in some use since about 1850. By 1870 it had replaced the old way of jigging by handline and shifted the chase from the comparatively shallow Bay of St. Lawrence in the Canadian Maritimes, the traditional haunt of the jiggers, to the coastal waters from Hatteras to the Gulf of Maine, where the greater depths were suitable for netting.

From the southward, where the vast schools first mysteriously surfaced, the schooner armada followed the migrating mackerel northward, up to fifty miles offshore initially, then as close in as a mile or two up around New Jersey and Long Island. Around June the fleet returned to port to leave off the first installment of its huge pickled catch (if lucky), to refit and set out again to the eastward for the summer fishery, pursuing the ever-restless mackerel until they disappeared back into the deep, as unaccountably as they had arisen, somewhere off the Maritimes in November. The Gloucester mackerel catch for 1881 was 163,851 barrels, or 32,770,200 pounds.

The focus of the previous spring's reawakening had been on the fast mackerel schooners with their spiking topmasts and clouds of canvas, off for southern climes under a fresh offshore westerly redolent of the blooming shad. Less carefree and more hazardous was the lot of the bankers fitting out at the adjoining wharves, dory-trawling for codfish on Western Bank and the nearer grounds, and for the long haul to the fog-ridden never-never world of the Grand Bank of Newfoundland in April that wouldn't release them home for Gloucester until August or September.

The bankers were the brutes of the Gloucestermen. They were the biggest, ranging up to 125 tons, gone for weeks and months at a time, not a little of it spent with cocked ears and straining eyes in the undeviating track of the transatlantic steamships.

Such long trips to nowhere demanded capacity. Out with salt, bait, ice and stores, back with the kenches, or bins, in the fish hold stuffed to the overhead with stenching salt-split codfish. The schooner *Herman Babson*, Captain Charlie Lawson, arrived from the Grand Bank one memorable day in 1878 with the second largest fare on record to that date, 300,000 pounds of dressed codfish in his hold. And to think that every hook had been baited by hand, every dory hoisted, swung over the rail and rowed out by back power, every mile of trawl set by hand, every struggling fish dragged up from the bottom by hand, hove up into the dory and rowed back to the *Babson* and pitched aboard, and split, and gibbed, and washed, and flung below, and salted, and kenched, and sailed into Gloucester, and pitched up on the wharf, by everlasting hand.

On the summer salt bankers and mackerel seiners they broke in the boys and the greenhorns, broke 'em in easy.

By October, most generally, the bankers had finished their season and were back in Gloucester, and the mackerelers were not far behind. The most weatherly of both (schooners and men) were now refitted for the haddock fishery that got under way in November, dory-trawling, right through the winter until the following April. During the late fall the haddockers worked the outside of Massachusetts Bay, and then, as the fish moved offshore, the larger vessels followed them out to sea as far as Georges and vicinity.

The haddockers were market fishermen, running short trips of only a few days, constantly on the go between the grounds and Boston, usually, with iced fish, with no apparent regard for the weather. In a good year, such as the winter of 1880–81, the Gloucester haddockers stocked 350,000 pounds per vessel on the average.

Of the remainder of the fleet that by the onset of winter wasn't off to the eastward halibuting and to the Georges for cod and haddock, the vessels unfit for the worst the Western Ocean could be counted on to dish up were laid up until spring. The rest were employed in coasting, perhaps, or were sent off with short crews to Newfoundland to bring back frozen bait (with dire warnings not to get frozen in themselves) — herring, mainly, caught by the hardy, independent and not always friendly (when they suspected the Yanks of fishing for *their* herring) "herring-chokers," as the Gloucestermen characterized the Newfies when there happened not to be one in the crew.

Thus it was that the hardest-worked vessels and men were pretty constantly at it, most all the year round, in and out of as many as three or four fisheries. The fitting-out process was a fine art in itself, as important to a schooner's success, and safety, as the skill and endurance of the men and the mood of the fish; most of all, it told the world what kind of a skipper she had.

Every prudent master hauled or beached his charge at least twice a year to inspect the hull below the waterline, the rudder, the caulking in the seams, the fastenings, to look for signs of damage or rot to keel or planking, to scrape away the colonies and gardens of marine growth that had attached themselves to the hull in the months at sea or lying in the dock since the previous paint job, and to repaint the bottom with a few gallons of the copper antifouling compound developed at the red landmark Tarr and Wonson paint factory out on the seaward point of Rocky Neck, guaranteed to restore a knot or two to the mossiest of flyers.

If bottom repairs were needed, hauling on one of the six steam-operated marine railways was in order — Burnham's or Parkhurst's down on Duncan's Point or Rocky Neck's pair on Smith Cove. If only minor work or a quick between-the-tides paint job could be gotten away with, the vessel occasionally was warped up into the head of the dock and grounded upright or on her bilges, saving the expense of towing charges and lay-days on the railways.

Ballasting was next on the master's mind. Without ballast, your Gloucesterman, like any other sailboat, would navigate about as well upside down as rightside up. Unlike displacement yachts, with outside iron or lead on their keels, the Gloucester schooners depended for their stability on ballast stowed deep down in the hold. Stone was the cheapest and handiest until the end of the nineteenth century, when pig iron, taking less space for the weight, came into more widespread use. *Pig*, incidentally, is a fisherman's hoodoo, never uttered aboard; so 'twas "hog" iron.

The ballast was packed in about amidships, fore and aft of the mainmast, under the heavily planked floor of the fish hold in an effort to prevent it from shifting and capsizing the vessel in the event of a knockdown by sea or squall. The fine distribution of the ballast, and cargo and stores for that matter, was crucial to sailing trim, some doing better down by the head, others a little by the stern.

The quantity of ballast varied with the burthen of the vessel, the fishery, and the intuition of the skipper. Relative to their displacement, the hard-driven haddockers carried the most: a fifty-tonner might stow up to thirty-five tons of ballast and another six of ice besides. The fresh halibuters and Georgesmen carried about half their displacement in ballast, with relatively more ice, being away on longer trips. The summer mackerel seiners loaded in the least, twenty tons in a sixty-ton schooner plus a great quantity of salt. The bankers, on the other hand, rarely sailed with permanent ballast, relying almost entirely on a deadweight of salt and a heavy cache of fresh water and stores outward, a full fare of salt fish coming home.

A lowly factor, ballast, but essential to the formula of Gloucester's supremacy in an unusual respect: half a million tons, say, of the smoothest, roundest, sea-worn stones imaginable on Cape Ann's ocean shore a mile or two at most from the hungry holds of the fleet. Not hard to handle, as stone goes, and almost easy to keep clean. Farmer Isaac Patch on Eastern Point worked a thriving business on the side, loading his ox carts with the "pobbles" from his High Pobbles Beach and Grapevine Cove on the crashing Atlantic shore of his property and rattling them over the dirt road across the Point to the ballast docks at the harbor.

Later, in the 1870s and on, Ike's neighbor, farmer George Marble Wonson, refined the business into high technology. Old Man Wonson put up on Rockport's Cape Hedge a warehouse of hundred-ton capacity, its roof connected to adjacent Pebbly Beach by a trestle. A steam donkey engine hauled the laden two-and-a-half-ton cars up the track to the heights, where the round rocks were dumped into the scuttle. Lighters sailed or steamed

FITTING OUT TIME

round from Gloucester to the jutting wharf; the chutes were opened, and the pobbles thundered down into the battered ballast boxes on deck. Or the rocks were hauled overland to the wharves by Wonson's caravan of horse-drawn tip carts.

When demand ran high in the winter, Farmer Wonson's crews fought banks of snow, dikes of sea ice and gales of wind to supply the needs not only of the Gloucestermen but of the giant, high-sided salt ships that dared not brave the return crossing to Europe too light after ladling out their cargoes to the world's thirstiest consumer of sodium chloride. Winters were not the only hazards. Wonson's old schooner, the *William H. Baylies*, sprang a leak while loading off the Cape Hedge wharf one August day in 1873 and sank on the spot — like a stone, and irrecoverably. They saved the sails and rigging. Loss $800, uninsured, plus innumerable rocks returned to the deep.

While supervising his ballasting, the Gloucester skipper of the 1880s had a hundred and one other matters on his mind, from the soundness of his pawl bitt to the state of his medicine chest. If bound for Georges summer-fishing, he could afford to sport his maintopmast and jibboom; if facing the winds of winter, he left both ashore and sailed off "snug-rigged" under his lowers. If mackereling summers in a yachtsman's breeze, he sent up main and fore topmasts, ran out the jibboom and flew every blessed stitch of sail she'd carry.

And then there was the rigging — standing and running, shrouds and stays, lanyards and halyards, downhauls and outhauls, topping lifts, pendants, dory tackle, vangs and sheets to check for wear or chafe, and chafing gear. And blocks: inspect the cheeks for splits and the pins for wear, and grease the sheaves, and check your shackles too, for the proverbial chain is as strong as the weakest link. Masts to be slushed down and examined for checks, crosstrees to be painted, mast hoops, gaff jaws, and parrals to be looked over, and boom jaws and topping lift sheave pins while you're at it. Pumps. Deck and house leaks. Water butts to clean. Windlass and steering gear to grease.

Sails. That cotton duck, the winter suit, some of it thick and stiff as the heaviest cardboard. Look for mildew, for chafe, for the little tears that explode into big rips, for pulled stitches, worn bolt ropes and cringles, missing reef points — and off to the loft with them.

Ever at the fore with all hands, not the least the owners, was the condition of the ground tackle. That anchor to windward, dug into the mud against every gale that blows, holding you off the crashing shoals of Georges, holding you off that roaring lee shore, or just holding the halibuter where the dorymen left her before a "thick-'o-fog," as they called the thickest of 'em, or snow squall shut her off from sight and sound.

Halibuters carried the mightiest ground tackle of all — three momentous anchors of 675 pounds each, beat out on the forges of the Cape Ann Anchor

Works, at that time down on Vincent's Point at the harbor, and as much as 425 fathoms, half a mile, of manila cable up to nine inches in circumference, almost three inches in diameter, every foot of it no better than every flaw. The bankers carried the same size anchors and cable, but less of the latter, while the Georgesmen put their faith in lighter gear on both counts. Haddockers were equipped with cable stowed to port and chain to starboard. The mackerel seiners, rarely coming to anchor unless they had to, left their cable ashore and took chain alone. Chain was backbreaking to raise at the windlass, once overboard, while manila was merely the devil; a wet cable tying a Gloucester halibuter to the bottom of The Gully between Western and Banquereau weighed in at four tons, plus anchor.

Years back, the town had produced its own cordage from two ropewalks, long gone now, one that extended 750 feet between Middle and Prospect streets, a few feet west of the present Sawyer Free Library, the other a landmark above Pavilion Beach for 625 feet to the west of the very fancy summer hotel, the Pavilion.

From davits to dories each of the Gloucester fisheries had its own ways, tried, and, as often as Dame Fortune smiled, true. The halibut-catchers carried six big dories, fifteen feet long on the bottom (as dories are measured), nested and lashed on deck bottoms-up while on passage, three to a side; miles of trawls, thousands of hooks in dozens of tubs, the deck area between the masts partitioned by "checkerboards" for the reception of fresh-caught halibut philosophically awaiting dismemberment. Bankers also carried half a dozen of these "double dories" and lighter trawls, but no "checkers," only splitting tables set up abaft the main rigging when a deck of fish demanded dressing. Haddockers favored smaller dories, fourteen feet on the bottom, built especially for the fishery, deeper and beamier. The handlining Georgesmen left port with but a single dory, swung from the stern davits; the crew slatted off their catch back over the rail and into "gurry pens" on the deck behind them.

The mackerel schooner was the most specialized, carried the most paraphernalia, fitted for the most temperamental of the fisheries. If she had been otherwise engaged, the decks must be cleared, the heavy seine roller rigged on the port quarter rail and the outrigger near the port forerigging to hold the seineboat off when towing alongside. The seineboats, thirty-four or thirty-six feet long and designed for fast rowing and capacity, must be hauled out of dry storage in some field up back, repaired, no doubt, caulked here and there, painted and put overboard — the Gloucester expression for launching a small boat; the big mackerel schooners often towed a pair of seineboats and a pair of seines, large and small for deep and shoal sets, and two dories, which made quite a procession.

Higgins and Gifford were far and away the leading builders of seineboats, surfboats and whaleboats, besides dories and small workboats and yachts.

The partners moved to East Gloucester from Cape Cod in 1871 and figured that in their first four years their boats, set bow to stern, would stretch two and a half miles. The seineboat is characteristically sharp forward for rowing and being towed, whereas the whaleboat from which it developed was sharper aft, for backing off fast from an angry harpooned whale. Higgins and Gifford abandoned the lapstrake method of planking soon after their arrival in Gloucester and built their new seineboats smooth-sided, rendering them stronger, faster and less liable to snag the twine. Hard used, the boats lasted only six or seven years.

As the day of sailing approached, salt was taken on. Not for nothing was Gloucester known as the saltiest port in the world. The Georgesmen and the bankers, above and beyond the vagaries of the fresh fish market as they were, brought home salt codfish, one of the staples of the world's diet in every country and every clime, and hove out around the Point on every return trip with as many as 300 hogsheads of salt stashed below as interim ballast. Likewise the seiners on their longer trips, with anywhere from 175 to 500 barrels below, a third of them filled with salt as ballast, the lot to be jammed to the heads with pickled mackerel (all hands hoped) for the passage home. Additionally, the bait that wasn't iced or frozen had been salted to prevent spoilage. Finally there were the demands of fisheries too distant for the fresh market, such as the Greenland halibut, the surplus caught by fresh halibuters when they ran out of ice and halibut caught incidentally by the salt fishermen, all of which was steaked, or flitched, brought home and sold to the smokehouses.

As if all this weren't savor sufficient, most of the multimillions of pounds of fish landed every year in Gloucester had been "slack-salted" aboard with the minimum required for preservation. Ashore, these acres of fish were washed and resalted for drying in the sun on the flakes or pickled or canned or smoked, and the salt consumption overall was perfectly staggering. Gloucester's salt was poured in by mammoth, square-rigged iron barques and ships and occasional steamers from Cadiz in Spain (the most favored, though the debate was endless), Trapani in Sicily (preferred by many for codfish on long trips), Liverpool (for pickling mackerel and herring) and sometimes the Caribbean.

Something over 43 million pounds of the white stuff was landed in Gloucester in 1879. Twenty-eight years later, by 1907, salt fish was in such world demand that ten steamers unloaded more than 64 million pounds. That's 32,000 tons. No matter the odds, either. The salt must go through. In January of 1906 the British salt barque *Ednyfed*, 1115 tons, arrived in Gloucester Harbor *116 days* out of Trapani, long since given up for lost. Encountering terrific gales and head winds, the *Ednyfed* had beaten to within three hundred miles of Cape Cod on her fifty-seventh day out, only to be driven back by storms, then doggedly recovered and fought on to weary victory. Bully for John Bull!

If not salt, then ice — one or the other in ships of wood before the days of freezers. Ice for refrigeration, and for the market fishery, got a great boost in 1876 when Francis Homans, in exuberant celebration of the Centennial, built the biggest icehouse in Massachusetts — 210 by 236 feet, with a capacity of 34,000 tons — in West Gloucester, dredged the adjoining swamp, dammed the stream and created Fernwood Lake for swimming and amusements for the public, ice for the fishing industry and a near monopoly for himself. The fishermen aboard and their cohorts ashore consumed only twenty-five thousand tons a year, which left almost ten thousand for the iceboxes of their wives. Besides, there was other ice to cut, in other ponds and lakes.

With the ice pens full, the hour of sailing pressed. As much fresh bait as obtainable was purchased and iced below. For the halibuter this meant mackerel, cod, haddock, hake or pogies (menhaden), or frozen herring in the wintertime; for the Georgesman, fresh or frozen herring, mackerel, alewives or pogies; while the bankers, always hard up for bait it seems, took what they could get from herring to mackerel, clams or squid — even gulls caught on a baited hook on the grounds. The haddockers were the finickiest: nothing would do but salt pogy.

And now the cook, so essential to the well-being of the foc'sle, more than crew and less than master (Gloucestermen shipped no mates) and paid to match, has come to life. Fresh water is useful aboard, and "the doctor," so called because he serves that function as well on occasion, besides qualifying in his own right frequently as a master mariner, hoists a bucket in the rigging as summons to the water boat to sail up alongside and fill his casks, some on deck, some below. Wood and coal for the stove in the main cabin, even in summer when the clammy fingers of a banks fog can creep with chill insinuation down the companionway, and for the Shipmate cookstove in his galley abaft the foremast and the fo'c'sle. A barrel of kerosene for the lamps.

As for the provisions, the cook on a Gloucester banker of seventy tons put aboard the following, complete, for fifteen men bound on a three-month dory-trawling trip to the Grand Bank of Newfoundland in the summer of 1879 — and "excellent fare" he made of them too, according to a scientific observer along for the ride:

Five barrels of beef, eight of flour, one each of pork, pigs knuckles, molasses, bean and dried apples, and a half barrel of hardtack crackers; ten bushels of potatoes, one each of rice, onions and dried peas, and a half bushel of oatmeal; 350 pounds of brown sugar, 200 of butter, 150 of lard, twenty each of Indian meal and tea, fifteen of coffee, five of saleratus, two pounds each of pepper, mustard and ginger, a pound each of hops, cloves and cassia, and a half pound of nutmeg; four boxes each of raisins and sage; three bags of table salt; twelve papers of corn starch; forty-eight packages of baking powder; forty-eight cans of condensed milk; and twenty-four bottles of essence of lemon.

The last item, loaded with the then unidentified antiscorbutic vitamin C, was presumably on board for the benign purpose — already amply demonstrated in lemons and limes — of warding off scurvy, the mariner's bane; for of fresh fruit and green vegetables, the lack of which was the culprit in the dread disease, there was nary a trace, cook doubtless aware from long experience that his vessel would make a couple of baiting trips in to the barren shores of Newfoundland, and lucky to find bait, never mind greens.

And now the men have kissed good-bye to their wives and their children and their girl friends and their mothers, or been collared out of the saloon by the Old Man, and are swinging or swaying down Duncan (or "Drunken," as the locals called it) Street to the wharf with their seabags.

Yon Gloucesterman tugs at the springlines, the weather is fair, or likely foul, and 'tis time to be off for the banks.

1

🕊 *1.* Bound for fitting-out at Gloucester, the *Henry Ford* wound up on Coffin's Beach instead when the towline snapped. It took three tugs and five days to float the beached leviathan, providing a famous Marblehead yacht designer time to get there with his camera. (L. Francis Herreshoff, Thomas Collection)

🕊 *2.* The King of the Mackerel Killers, Captain Sol Jacobs, lost no time getting the sticks into his latest enthusiasm, Gloucester's first big auxiliary schooner, the *Helen Miller Gould*. Launched from Bishop's on March 29, 1900, she was sparred, rigged, canvased and properly fitted-out in just thirteen days, and here she is on her trial trip past the end of Eastern Point to Beverly and back on April 11, with 150 or so celebrants on deck. Next day she was off for mackerel. Eighteen phenomenally successful months later, on October 25, 1901, the *Gould*'s gasoline engine caught fire off Nova Scotia and she burned to the waterline, fortunately with no loss of life. Lesson in nomenclature: her sails, starting from aft, are mainsail; above that, main topsail; then foresail; fore topsail above; fisherman's staysail, the trapezoid between the masts; just ahead of the foremast, the boomed jumbo jib or forestaysail; the jib, from end of bowsprit to the head of the foremast; and finally, the balloon jib, ballooner, jib topsail or flying jib, depending upon what the skipper calls it. (Ernest L. Blatchford, Thomas Collection)

2

1. Joseph Call's spar shop at Vincent's Cove in the 1880s. Sparmakers were kept busy with new vessels and replacing sticks lost at sea in a gale of wind. Perhaps the owner himself, so popular they named the tug *Joe Call* for him, leans against what looks to be a mainmast squared off at the head to take the type of hardware (already being fitted on the foremast at left) that will secure the squared-off foot of the lighter topmast, on the sawhorses farthest to the right. Other light spars such as gaffs are being worked on. The bowsprit, probably, hangs from the rafters. Lying on the rough-hewn timber against the left wall is a gaff jaw. Spars were of white pine until the biggest trees began to give out, then of fir or yellow pine. The mainmast of the great racing fisherman *Columbia* was ninety-three feet long and nineteen and three-quarters inches in diameter at the height of the main boom, which stretched aft seventy-eight feet. When the time for stepping came, the customer tied up to the spar wharf. The mast was trundled out, hoisted up to the vertical between the poles of a high and mighty shears and then gently lowered through the deck until the tenoned heel slipped into the framework above the keelson called the step. (The Smithsonian Institution)

2. Ben Colby's sail loft on Leighton's wharf, about 1912, eighteen sailmakers on the floor and a half a dozen competitors on the waterfront. Fifty-five years later and still cutting sails, apprentice Charlie Olsen, fifth from the right in the turtleneck, recalled that in those last hours of the heyday a whole row of 'em passed the duck of a schooner mainsail as thick as boot leather along their laps, and the man or boy who couldn't handstitch thirty feet of it an hour might as well start looking for another line of work. In 1899 the Gloucester sailmakers won three dollars from the bosses for a nine-hour day after a three-week strike. (Courtesy of Edith Olsen)

3. BIG anchors, from the Cape Ann Anchor Works. (Ernest L. Blatchford, Thomas Collection)

2

3

1

1. And small anchors, from Ben Frazier. There were twenty-four blacksmith shops in Gloucester in 1880. (Cape Ann Historical Association)

2. Barrels (or butts). (Cape Ann Historical Association)

3. And more butts (or barrels). Gloucester packers alone in 1880 used 150,000 barrels and 400,000 wooden boxes, 450 pounds of fish to a box. (Stereopticon view, Cape Ann Historical Association)

4. Wood for the galley stove. (Martha Hale Harvey, Thomas Collection)

2

3

4

1. Water for the cook. Captain Cleaves sails the water sloop *Aqua Pura*, one of several in Gloucester, on a well advertised mission across harbor. The hand pump and hose are amidships. "In Gloucester the water is purchased from an *aquarius*, who plies about the harbor in a boat called the *Aqua pura*," wrote Henry Osborn of the start of his dory-trawling trip to the Grand Bank in 1879. "The hold of this boat is one immense tank, filled from the city hydrants, and from it the water is pumped into the barrels of the schooner. Judging from the taste of the water and the untidy appearance of the *Aqua pura*, one might think that the waterman was not quite as neat about his water tanks as could be desired. In fact, to a landsman the water he supplied was absolutely disgusting. . . ." In fact, the writer was too kind. Gloucester got along without a municipal water and sewerage system for another six years and in 1879 relied on wells and outhouses that were no farther from them than was convenient. (Ernest L. Blatchford, Thomas Collection)

2. The Italian salt ship *Yallaroi* discharges at Pew's salt wharf in August 1914, just as World War I is breaking out in Europe. Main yards are cocked to make room for the schooner alongside taking on salt. A tub filled by the lumpers in *Yallaroi*'s hold has been hoisted out by a tackle hauled by the deck engine on the steam lighter *Eagle*, lying outside the schooner, and is dumping into a chute hung between the davits down to the Gloucesterman's open hatch. When offloading into Pew's storage shed, the tubs were swung over to the high platforms projecting out from the building and spilled into the waiting wheelbarrows of the stevedores. *Yallaroi* grossed 1565 tons, was 245 feet long, drew 22 feet of water and doubtless had been partially lightened at anchor on the "Deep Hole" a little farther out in the harbor before being towed to Pew's, one of the few deep water wharves in the port.

The other large salt wharf was William Parsons's in East Gloucester, where a ship and a barque had been unloading on two sides, while three schooners lay abreast against the third, on December 9, 1872. It came on to blow a screeching gale during the night, surging all that great weight up against the wharf every which way, until the next morning the vast shed, 120 by 55 feet, was trembling and swaying so alarmingly that the workmen were ordered out. And just in time. With the crack of a thunderbolt the entire floor collapsed and dropped 2500 tons of salt, 10,000 hogsheads of it, into the dock below with a splash that must have been something to see — along with 40,000 pounds of fish. (Chester N. Walen, Thomas Collection)

1

57

58

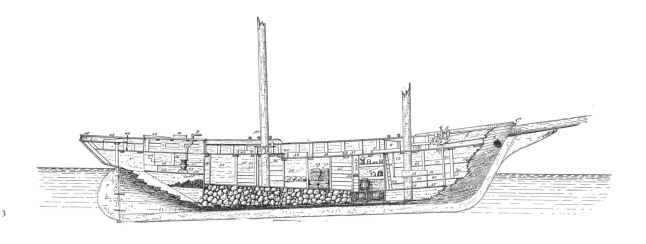

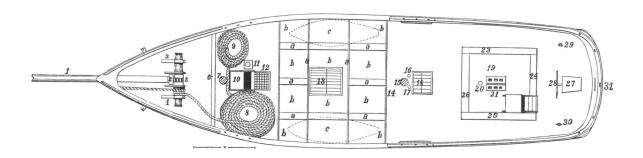

1. Up comes a tub of Turk's Island salt from the hold of the three-masted Nova Scotian schooner *J.L. Ralston* at Pew's wharf, 1920. Thirsty work down there, as attested by the raised water jug. (Gordon W. Thomas, Thomas Collection)

2. Baiting up for the shore fishery around 1900, the crew of a Gloucester dory trawler prepares to sail on a short trip with quick sets and a fast return for both the fresh and salt fish markets. When all baited, the skate by the rail will be replaced in the tub. (Ernest L. Blatchford, Thomas Collection)

3. Sectional drawing of a Gloucester halibut schooner of the 1880s by Captain Joseph W. Collins, from the stern, outlining the after cabin with coal bin under floor, stone ballast under the fish holds which are divided into pens that fill with fish as the ice is depleted. Next forward are the fore hold, freshwater casks stowed deep below the cook's heavy and small stores, the forecastle steps from the companionway, galley, foremast and forecastle with table, berths and lockers.

The deck plan from the bow shows the windlass (2–5), jib sheet traveler (6), foremast (7), anchor cables (8 & 9), forecastle companionway (10), galley stovepipe (11), fore hatch grating (12), main hatch (13), checkers or deck pens (b) and nested dories (c). Aft of the break in the deck (14) are the mainmast (15), pumps (16 & 17), after hatch (18), cabin house or trunk (19), stovepipe (20), skylight (21), bait-cutting planks (23–26), wheelbox and wheel (27 & 28) and main sheet bitts (29 & 30). (Goode's *Fisheries*)

1

1. Getting under way, half the gang is on the throat halyard raising the mast end of the gaff, commonly rove through a deck block to port of the foremast, the rest hauling away behind the rising foresail on the gaff's peak halyard to starboard. (Albert Cook Church, The Whaling Museum)

2. Whistling for a breeze, the banker *Louise R. Sylva*, a 116-foot McManus design built by Tarr and James in 1904, lies listless in the stream. Sail patches reveal the usual points of chafe and strain: the clews of the ballooner and jib where they thrash across the stays when coming about; the luff of the foresail against the after fore shroud when sailing before the wind; from head to clew of the mainsail where the topping lift slats constantly along the cloth. The *Sylva* stranded at Newfoundland on a voyage for herring in 1928 and broke up; the crew was saved. (Eben Parsons, Cape Ann Historical Association)

3. For want of a breeze the skipper picks up a tow from one of the Gloucester tugs that shepherds his vessel out of the crowded inner harbor past Rocky Neck and the landmark copper bottom paint factory, there since 1863, until a breath of wind is felt or the long hawser is called for. (Thomas Collection)

2

3

🐦 *1.* Still no wind. Past Rocky Neck and coming up on Ten Pound Island, this large clipper schooner, off for the fishing grounds, has cast off the short lines and now glides along behind the chugging tug on the faster long tow to the outer harbor and beyond Eastern Point, if necessary, to slat around and wait for some air. (Herman W. Spooner, Thomas Collection)

🐦 *2.* For want of a towboat (or too tight to pay the charge), skipper may just suggest that all hands take to the dories for a "Nova Scotia tow" — a practice not entirely unknown at Gloucester, though rarely if ever photographed. Such back work was even more the order of the day with the Newfies, here sweating the *D.J. Thornhill* out of St. John's, Newfoundland, through a flat calm. (Mystic Seaport Museum)

🐦 *3.* A gentle westerly is just enough to fill the sails of the *Admiral Dewey*, bound halibuting. The *Dewey* was built by Tarr and James, in '98, naturally. The two out on the bowsprit are attending to some kind of rigging problem, maybe with the balloon downhaul. These pole bowsprits, and their even longer predecessors fitted with the fixed extensions, similar in purpose to topmasts, called jibbooms, were the death of many the fisherman struggling with a flogging headsail in a gale of wind while being regularly (and irregularly) plunged over his head into a raging sea. To make matters worse, the footropes on which one of the pair is standing, net lines and bowsprit shrouds leading back to the bow were too often the object of sloppy maintenance and would give way when most needed. Hence the term "widowmakers" for bowsprits, moving Tom McManus in 1902 to invent the first knockabout schooner that got along with no bowsprit at all, the jibs leading down to the foredeck. (Ernest L. Blatchford, Thomas Collection)

62

2

1. Frequently the wind freshens coming out of the west onto Gloucester Harbor from across Stage Fort and Cressy's Beach, and here the new and fast Tarr and James clipper *Dauntless* — possibly bound for Newfoundland for a cargo of bait herring, since she carries only two dories and a short crew — catches a smart breeze about abreast of them. Three more hitches should get her clear of Eastern Point's Dog Bar and out to sea. (Ernest L. Blatchford, Thomas Collection)

2. Almost out of Gloucester Harbor now, and in the steady grip of the southeasterly, the handsome flyer *Saladin* — another beauty off the Tarr and James ways in 1902 — clips along with everything flying. She's bound mackereling, one seineboat towing, the other and the dory on deck, and she looks brand new, maybe even on her maiden trip, for the grand spread of canvas is as pristine as can be. (Robert W. Phelps, Martin Horgan Collection)

3. A bone in her teeth, as the saying goes, *Tattler* is clear of the harbor and the Point and off for the eastward dory handlining. *Tattler* was the talk of the fleet in her day, built by Arthur D. Story in 1901, one of the biggest schooners ever to sail out of Gloucester at 172 tons. On September 6, 1916, Captain Alden Geele brought *Tattler* home with half a million pounds of salt fish, stocking $21,000. It was the largest trip and stock in the records of the dory handline fishery. (Ernest L. Blatchford, Thomas Collection)

3

65

≋ Rail under to her main sheerpoles, the great *Columbia* smashes through the seas offshore in a rare photograph taken on a fishing voyage in the early 1920s. (Charles Sayle Collection)

4. OFF FOR THE BANKS

Theirs is a life of toil, and although fortune smiles upon them occasionally and sends a good school of fish, yet they spend hours and hours at the rail, in the bitter cold of winter, waiting for a bite — "grubbing" as it is termed — with a family at home, whom they love as well as anyone loves his own; and the bread of this family depending upon the catch of fish . . . a continual grappling with the elements, a struggle for life, with storm and old ocean in its anger to meet; and with pluck and daring they wring success from the very verge of the grave.

— *George H. Procter*

Patience is a cardinal virtue with fishermen, of Gloucester as everywhere and always. In the old days, when the start of a fishing trip hung on the whimsical wind and the willful weather, a man's patience could be tried long before he got to the banks — before ever he left the harbor. If you don't like the weather, as the old saw about the New England variety goes, wait a minute. Likewise the wind.

A visiting Norwegian fisheries expert, Frederick M. Wallen, hooked a ride mackereling in the old schooner *William S. Baker* in the mid-1870s. The night was dark, raining and foggy as he sloshed down to the wharf and boarded the *Baker*, rather unpropitiously, he thought. Next morning they cast loose in not a breath of air, and the tide carried them out into the stream of the inner harbor, where they dropped their anchor to avoid drifting ashore.

"While we waited for the wind," he recalled, "a portion of the crew passed away the time by taking a bath and swimming out in the deep. Their invitation to me to swim a race with them I was in the notion of accepting, when the signal was given to make sail and get under way. All came on board, took off their swimming clothes, and caught hold at the anchor-breaking and later at the hauling-out so that it was a pleasure to see them."

One never knew. A green hand signed on in June 1859 for a mackereling trip to the Bay of St. Lawrence aboard the schooner *Samuel Gilbert*, which was hauled out on Parkhurst's railway for painting when he came down and joined in, getting about as much on himself as on the vessel's bottom.

The *Gilbert* was launched and brought to anchor in the stream while last-minute stores were rowed out and put aboard and a last-minute cook signed on. Next morning "we up anchor cheerily and stood out of the harbor in good style. Two or three others who had got under way earlier and owing to a lack of wind spent much time in dodging and beating about without much headway. Not so us — a fortunate dash of wind took us out to the Point in two long tacks, overtaking our friends who had the start, and rounding the light handsomely in company with several other Baymen."

One can just hear the catcalls from the deck of the *Samuel Gilbert* as their dash of wind carried them past their rivals. Peculiarities of Gloucester Harbor, those dashes of wind scurrying surreptitiously off the land during the warm seasons, filling one sail here and dashing and dancing off with it, while another not a hundred yards away hangs as limp and long-faced as a wallflower.

Until the first steam towboat appeared in Gloucester not much before 1869, with the wind was the only way of getting under way, unless the men took to the dories and towed their vessel from berth to berth or out to the anchorage as a deservedly unpopular last resort. If the glass was falling fast, or if it was blowing too hard even for the captain's liking, or if the fog was so thick that from the wheel he couldn't make out the bowsprit, or if the vessel was frozen in the ice right solid, of if there *was* no wind, no one was going anywhere.

The advent of those squat and busy little helpers, engines throbbing, plumes of smoke and steam trailing off to leeward, wrought a minor revolution around the waterfront. Now anything that floated dead in the water without the wind could be pulled, pushed, nudged, edged, elbowed, hauled, coaxed, bullied or backed from the launching at Essex to the fitting-out at Gloucester, from berth to berth to railway to salt wharf to ice wharf and back, to anchorage, to the breakwater in search of a breeze, even to Boston if called for. Break ice too. And haul off wrecks.

The tugs put legs on the harbored fleet. They hustled it no end. For thirty years they did Gloucester's homework, made it twice the port with their busy chugging, helped boost it to the heights before the first auxiliary engines turned up in the schooners and gradually put the scurriers out of business.

For the 250 years before the Industrial Revolution discovered Gloucester, though, it was all wind. The distance is not much under three miles almost due southwest from the wharves to the open Atlantic, which dampens the sultry breath of the prevailing wind of summer on this coast. Your typical "smoky sou'wester," however, blows true only when encountered somewhat offshore, away from the influence of the warm air mass over the land that alongshore tends to deflect it to a more westerly, offshore, squally slant.

A vessel sailing out of Gloucester Harbor in the face of the sou'wester encounters the air "dashing" off the mainland shore quite favorably to a close reach. At other times, when the outer harbor lies glazed in a flat, glassy calm, the knowing helmsman makes for the Eastern Point shore, where he is pretty liable to find a few easterly "cat's-paws" dashing off the peninsula's slim land mass to assist his craft in ghosting along while all others drift helplessly about.

And so it is that at all seasons of the year the lightest of airs from most any quarter is enough to help or challenge a sailing vessel to run, reach or beat out of Gloucester. Once outside a few miles, the larger weather takes over and frees the sailor from the whims of the coastal zephyrs — or condemns him to a windless night.

Only against a flat-out, hissing no'theaster (always no'theaster in Gloucester, never "nor'easter"), or a feather-white nor'wester (always nor'wester, never "no'thwester") hellbent from Montreal, does sail alone make hard weather of it working in around the seething seas off the Point, up the rollicking, surging length of the outer harbor to the safe haven behind Ten Pound Island and its welcome light. Patience makes all bearable.

When embarking right from the wharf, the outbound schooner is warped around by her docking lines until headed into the stream, if she isn't already pointing that way, and the skipper orders the mainsail up. All hands jump to, straining on the halyards rove through the deck blocks as if in a tug-o'-war with that huge crumple of canvas hung from the great main gaff, half the gang on the throat of it, half on the peak hauling in twice the line with twice the purchase — HEAVE, ugh . . . HEAVE, ugh . . . HEAVE, ugh — men and blocks groaning as the spar, thick as the City Hall flagpole, and unfurling sail inch skyward up the mast. The breeze catches the rising expanse of duck, and our schooner slides away from the wharf in swirling whirlpools as the men move to raise the foresail, which after the monstrous main is duck soup.

Much the same routine is followed raising sail from out in the anchorage, where the vessel may have been moved to make way for another at the wharf or taken directly from the railway, as the *Samuel Gilbert* was. Up with mainsail, then foresail, and as she creeps forward on the anchor and the cable comes slack, the crew pitches in on the windlass brakes. *Clack, clack, clack,* the manila as heavy as a firehose snakes aboard, dripping, through the hawse pipe, foot by foot. Fetches up taut, nearly vertical, and they can feel the anchor break out of the mud only three or four fathoms below.

Free of the bottom, the schooner's head sags off as the wind catches her. The rest of the cable is hove in, easier now, and the anchor thumps up to the bow and is catted and washed down with buckets of seawater to douse the mud off amidst much shouting and peering over the rail. Skipper has ordered the staysail up, and up it flaps, the easiest yet.

She's regained headway just in time to be brought about under the Rocky

69

Neck shore with not much open water to spare. Up with the jib, thrashing most lively as one of those dashes comes flicking flat across the water from Stage Head. A short tack to the west'ard broad off Pavilion Beach. "Ready about!" yells the Old Man. The helmsman whirls his wheel hard down to port, spoke by spoke and hand over hand. She turns slowly into the wind, every sail flapping furiously but the jib, which is held to wind'ard till the last minute to help her around, and then she swings off.

The sails fill, the jib is let go, all sheets are started, and she's off and gathering headway again, headreaching to the sou'wester, picking up knots, an easy cant to the deck now, full and by, harbor gurgling off astern, the end of the Point and the open Atlantic up ahead.

No better acount of the typical first day at sea of a Gloucesterman a hundred years ago exists than that penned by Captain Joseph W. Collins in the log of the schooner *Marion,* off for the Grand Bank of Newfoundland fresh-halibuting on January 24, 1879. Not long afterward he embarked on his productive career with the United States Fisheries Commission.

It being understood that we should sail today, the boys all put in an appearance at the wharf between 8 and 9 a.m., many of them bringing under their arms a small calico bag containing a small supply of clean clothes for the trip, and nearly all getting a quantity of tobacco and pipes at the store; the order to the clerk generally being as follows: "Say, Archie, give us two pound terbaccer and a half dozen T.D.'s" (the common clay pipes with "T.D." marked on the bowl).

A noticeable absence of shore clothes, the hasty running for this and that article forgotten until the last moment, and the pulling here and hauling there, gave evidence that a "start" was contemplated.

In the meantime the cook built a fire in his cooking stove and began making preparations for dinner.

All were ready at last, and just before noon the sails were hoisted and we filled away from the wharf. As the city clock struck twelve we passed the "Fort," beating out of the harbor with a moderate southwest breeze.

After passing Eastern Point, at the harbor's mouth, we set the staysail and shaped our course E. by S. for the Banks, and so as to pass several miles to the southward of Cape Sable, Nova Scotia.

In the meantime the ropes were coiled, dories turned bottom up and securely lashed, and the vessel pumped out; while our ears, as we turned the "Point," were pleasantly greeted by the clang of the cook's dinner bell, calling us away from "straightening things up on deck." The crew is divided into two gangs for meals, the table in the forecastle not being large enough to accommodate all. One of the second gang now came aft saying, "I'll keep her along, skipper, while you get dinner"; whereupon I gave up the wheel, which I had held since starting, and went with the first gang down to dinner.

For dinner we had the usual first meal at sea, which, hastily prepared, generally consists of boiled salt beef and potatoes, with biscuits, pilot-bread and butter, strong tea, and fried beefsteak. This bill of fare is very much changed as soon as the "doctor" (cook) has time to prepare a greater variety, and, though beefsteak or other fresh meat is rarely seen after the first few days out, the table is well provided with plenty of good raised bread, cakes, pies, duff, etc., and last, though not least, the finest fish are served up in a manner rarely equaled elsewhere.

After dinner the patent log was put out, a note made of the bearing and distance of the land, and then everybody was called aft to "thumb the hat" in order that the watch might be set. All hands stand around an inverted hat, taking hold of it so that their thumbs are on top of the rim. The skipper then turns away his head, and, reaching over, touches one of the thumbs, and then counts around from left to right any number previously decided upon. The first one that the count reaches has the first watch. The counting then begins at the next thumb with "one," and so on until each man knows his watch, and with the injunction, "Remember now, whom you call," the performance ends, and the one having the first watch takes the wheel.

On board of trawling vessels it is very common for dorymates to stand watch together on a passage, and in this case only half of the crew "thumb the hat," they choosing their mates to stand with them. After the watch was set most of the men turned in and took a nap, while one or two busied themselves ganging hooks, etc.

At 3 p.m., the wind having increased to a smart breeze, we took in the staysail, and gaff-topsail. At 5 p.m., barometer 30.15; smurry-looking under the sun. The wind increased some after 5, and the sea made up sharp.

A little before seven o'clock p.m. our vessel took a heavy lurch to leeward, sending her lee rail so far under that, when she straightened up, the deck was nearly full, and several buckets-ful came down the companion-way over the lower cabin door, which sets about 18 inches above the deck, wetting the bed-clothes in the lee bunks, and also the boots lying on the floor. This episode called forth exclamations more forcible than polite from the occupants of the lee bunks, and shouts of laughter from their companions who could only see the ludicrous side of the accident. The sea by this time had risen sharp and choppy, and so frequent were the lurches — the main boom often going under to the slings — that we soon after double-reefed the mainsail. This done, I went below for the night, giving the usual order to "call me if there is any change in the force or direction of the wind."

After the reefed mainsail was set we hauled the log and found that we had made an average of 10 knots since we passed Thacher's Island. Barometer at 8 p.m., 30.05. Strong breeze all the latter part of this p.m.

5. DORYMATES

Bound for the fishing banks to the eastward, every Gloucester skipper took his bearings from the twin lighthouses of Thacher's Island off the Rockport shore as he shaped his course into the open Atlantic, just as the pinpoint flashes from them guided him home to Cape Ann through the night.

With Thacher's astern, the self-taught navigator was on his own. He had his taffrail log trailing away in his wake, spinning off the knots to tell him how far he'd sailed; his compass boxed in the cabin house where he and the helmsman could see it, inside and out; his sextant or quadrant for getting a fix on the sun or a star when the weather relented; his chronometer and navigation tables for reckoning his position from his fix; his barometer; his charts; and his luck.

The needle of navigational ability could swing wildly. Some skippers were true as true out there on the vasty blue. Others not, leading Captain Joseph W. Collins to urge with some asperity that masters of fishing schooners in the 1880s be made subject to strict examination and licensure (of which there was none), citing instances of homebound Gloucestermen fetching land as far off the mark as the Chesapeake. And there were the Merlins of dead reckoning, the skippers who could sense by some occult divining beyond the ken of ordinary mortals wherever they were in the middle of the ocean, and sniff out the fish half a mile down and ten away.

The all-time dead reckoner was Captain Joseph P. Mesquita, the most famous of the Portuguese fishermen who emigrated to Gloucester from the Azores. Smoky Joe was fishing on the Grand Bank in a thick-o'-fog when a monstrous big freighter suddenly loomed up over his schooner and drifted to a stop with a jangle of bells and a backward churn of the screw.

"Can you give us your position?" her master called down through his megaphone from the bridge, slightly sheepishly.

"What! Ya got all dat damn gear up dare, an' yer runnin' roun' da damn ocean an' ya don' know ware yar at? Hol' on dare wun minnid."

Joe Meskeet told one of the gang to heave the lead. It splashed, and up it came. He took the lead and squinted at the mud stuck to the tallow in the

72

hollow end and rubbed the stuff between his fingers and put it to his lips, muttering "damn fool, damn fool." He checked the current and his chart.

"Here yar, mister," he boomed back in the direction of the dimly seen bridge way up there, and gave him his coordinates, and his course in the bargain, and went back fishing.

When the fog scaled up, they shot the sun from that big black freighter with all "dat damn gear" and found that Smoky Joe Meskeet and his taste of mud were half a mile off out of three thousand. So claimed the late Everett R. Jodrey, waterfront factotum, who always felt a good story deserved a flourish or two in the transmission.

Captain Mesquita and his men had a couple of other encounters with steamships so legendized that it is high time to sort out the facts, which are as follows:

The first of this remarkable mariner's two *Mary P. Mesquita*s was caught a few miles off Cape Ann in one of the worst blizzards of the century that set in on November 26, 1898. At the height of it, the crew gathered in prayer to the patron saint of the fishermen, and their skipper vowed that if they were delivered home alive he would lead them on Whitsunday in their oilskins from their wharf to the Church of Our Lady of Good Voyage on Portugee Hill; there they would quite literally "crown" him in the Azorean religious tradition — and so crowned he would be every Whitsunday thereafter for the rest of his days, and for the rest of his days he would distribute bread to the poor of Gloucester.

At almost that moment of supplication they spied through the storm what appeared to be a coal barge adrift. But it turned out, as they drew closer, to be white, and they were sure in those seconds before the snow shut in again that it was the Boston-Portland steamer, dismantled of her upper works and in dire distress. Whether it was she or not, the *Portland* disappeared thereabouts forever that day with 157 souls and gave her name to the gale. The *Mary P.* made it back to Gloucester, and the delivered were as good as their word.

Eleven months exactly passed. On October 27, 1899 the same *Mary P. Mesquita* was off fishing, jogging along in a dense fog at nearly the same spot in the ocean east of Cape Ann when there was a sudden and alarming crescendo of engine sounds. As unexpectedly they stopped. The gut-busting blast of a steamship whistle rent the air, and out of the thick, higher than their mastheads, rose the bow of an ocean liner. From the bridge the helmsman had as suddenly seen the sails of the schooner dead ahead, but not in time. The Cunarder *Saxonia*, just leaving Boston, plowed into the *Mary P.* and cut her in half. Joe Mesquita and his men got two dories over and jumped in; one upset as the *Saxonia* lowered her lifeboats. The halves of the schooner sank like stones. Luckily the sea was smooth. Smoky Joe and all but one of his crew of fifteen were rescued and taken on to England, where he cabled the good word back to Gloucester, which had given them up for lost since a battered dory bearing the name *Mary P. Mesquita* had washed ashore some miles away.

Eighty-three years later, let it be said, the pentecostal crowning of some member of the Portuguese community in Gloucester is as faithfully, and meaningfully, observed as ever.

Getting back to the fishing, and the ways of it, there were all kinds of signs that told the Joe Mesquitas where their old spot was out there under that expanse of ocean, where the fish damn well better be: the distance from this known position and the soundings on that course, the color of the water and the direction and strength of the current, the look of the waves and the feel of the bottom.

And when they figured they were just about there, they would announce matter-of-factly, "Here we are," suggest that the jib be doused and furled, anchor let go, cable stuck out till she bit up and "stradded" (bound with pleated rope strands called "strads") in the hawsepipe to prevent chafing, staysail dropped and furled, foresail dropped and furled, mainsail dropped and furled, and dories put over with gear. With riding sail set in place of the main for the sake of some steadiness in the seaway, your Gloucesterman was "gone to housekeeping," as they said.

Each dory was outfitted with two pairs of nine-foot ash oars, wooden thole pins in the gunwales serving as oarlocks, pole gaff, bailing scoop, a V-shaped wooden roller that clamped to the gunwale for hauling in the trawl, woolen nippers (fingerless mittens worn as protection against the twine), a knife and a dory plug, a bottom drain plug with a rope becket on the outside to loop an arm through if the boat overturned. Sometimes a jug of fresh water. Since the men were required to provide their own dory compasses, few did.

Halibuters carried a "hurdy-gurdy" in the dory, a simple winch that clamped athwartships between the bow gunwales aft of the roller, for cranking in the trawl, and a couple of "killer sticks" for whacking unphilosophical halibut on the nose. The bankers carried in the dory a smaller "gob stick" that they thrust down the throat of a codfish when necessary to work loose the hook. Mast and sail were rarely thrown in except in summertime.

The halibut trawl ground line of heavy tarred cotton twine was used in sections of 375 fathoms (2250 feet). Every fifteen feet a short becket was knotted on, to the other end of which was tied a lighter "ganging" line five feet long, ending in a hook. So there were 150 hooks to a section, one section to a tub or to a square of canvas called a skate that was wrapped and tied around the coil, four skates to one full halibut trawl, 600 hooks and 9000 feet, almost a mile and three quarters of it.

The codfish trawl of the bankers was lighter and shorter, about 1700 feet to a tub, with 300 smaller hooks on three-foot gangings. A tub of haddock trawl was around the same length, but with 500 even smaller hooks on two-foot gangings, six to eight tubs to a dory, so the haddockers might be up half the night baiting by lamplight.

Using bait boards to protect the cabin top, the men cut the bait into slivers of varying length, depending on the fishery, baited the hooks and recoiled the trawl with the hooks in the center. A fast man could bait five hundred hooks in half to three quarters of an hour.

The top dory was lifted out of the nest by tackles hung from the main and fore rigging and hooked into the bow and stern beckets (rope loops), pushed clear of the rail and lowered into the water. One dorymate jumped in and the other handed down the baited tubs of trawl, anchors, buoys and buoy lines, which was a pretty good trick when a sea was running, and dory and vessel were rising and falling four or five feet in opposite directions. Then the man on deck climbed over the rail and with split-second timing jumped in himself, and while the gang was hoisting out the next dory in the nest, the thwarts were jammed on over the clamps, thole pins inserted and painter cast off. They shoved clear of the schooner, bent to the oars and were off, successively, one dory after another from the anchored vessel, in all directions like the spokes of a wheel if there wasn't much wind, or like a fan to windward if there was.

It was a long pull to the start of the set, as much as two or three miles before the dorymates agreed to ship their oars and throw over the first anchor and buoy line, the beginning of the trawl marked by the black ball, a hoop of canvas above the keg buoy, painted black. The lad in the stern now commenced throwing, or flicking, the trawl off the top of the coil, using a short stick to avoid getting accidentally hooked as the ground line and gangings flew out, while his dorymate manned the oars. (On occasion, if it looked like an especially hard set against the breeze to windward, the skipper would order fewer dories out, with three men in each — two at the oars, the third throwing the trawl. Or two dories might set a single trawl from either end, meeting in the middle.)

Several tubs and a mighty long pull at the oars later, the trawl was all out. Over splashed the second anchor and buoy line and flagged keg, and then the long pull back to the schooner. Before rowing back out, the halibuters waited maybe two, maybe eighteen hours, sometimes several days if it was too rough to haul, for the fish to take the bait. The bankers after codfish ordinarily set overnight, rising at three or so for breakfast before returning to their lines.

Back at the outermost buoy (which might take some searching to find), the bow man pulled in the keg, buoy line, anchor and trawl over the roller, only bringing the hurdy-gurdy into play with a turn around the shaft when the load of halibut on the trawl was extra heavy. The halibut in those times of plenty ranged from 150 to 300 pounds and as long as seven feet (the biggest recorded was at least 700 pounds) and sometimes objected quite furiously to capture, thrashing about with violence and jerking the dory this way and that until tired enough to be brought alongside and smacked on the snout a few times with the killer stick. It is hard to imagine boating such an unwilling giant. The strength and endurance demanded of the dory fishermen are awesome to contemplate; even the codfish taken on one ordinary trip to the banks averaged forty-five inches in length.

The paradox of the bank dory is that the heavier it is loaded the more stable it becomes — down to a point, of course. The men were especially wary of capsizing in choppy seas before they had a good fare of fish aboard. It might take two or three hours to haul the entire trawl. The bankers particularly, if the fishing was good, would have to row back to the schooner with a doryful of up to 1800 pounds five or six times to finish with a single trawl, hollering "Dory!" as they bumped up alongside, bringing skipper and cook running to the rail.

In the face of that kind of fishing, and if the weather still favored, the exhausted dorymates frequently had no alternative after finishing with their first set but to proceed with a second baiting and a second set within twenty-four hours. All in a day's work that could amount to forty tubs of fish a dory — up to eight hundred pounds in the round to a tub, which would salt down on board, after dressing, to around three hundred. That's thirty-two thousand pounds of codfish off the hook for two men in a dory, and an uncommonly good day it would be. On the other hand, they might have ten fish to show for it.

If the sea was calm and the fish were biting down there, the second round trip to the schooner for the repeat baiting and set could be avoided by carrying along extra bait and underrunning the trawl, rebaiting the hooks as the fish were taken off and the line was fed back over, which meant all the more room for fish without the trawl aboard.

If the wind had backed around while they were hauling, or sprung up against them out of a calm, it could take hours and perhaps some luck, straining at the oars against wind and waves, barely making headway, to reach the schooner. A rescue mission for one or more dories in real trouble meant the long and lousy job of raising the anchor and was out of the question with only the skipper and cook left aboard, or at best with a couple of the dorymen already back. Mobility was a prime consideration out on the banks, for the purposes of rescue, if necessary, and because many skippers preferred picking up their dorymen to making them row back.

The answer, when possible — and anchoring could not always be avoided in rough weather any more than fishing could — was the "flying set," whereby the skipper, upon reaching his spot, jogged her along a little off the wind with jib held to windward. The dories were swung over the lee rail and dropped back by their painters to the quarter, where the men jumped in with their gear. The painter was cast off, then over with anchor and buoy practically in the vessel's wake; in this way they commenced setting their trawls to leeward at a right angle to the schooner's course, at intervals of about half a mile in a fishing pattern that might cover as many as eight square miles of ocean.

Newly arrived skippers testing the bottom for fish often would set flying initially to save the crew the heavy work of anchoring and reanchoring unnecessarily. The maneuver had a certain flair to it and was standard procedure with the harddriven haddockers, allowing the men the easier job of hauling to leeward right off, and in the process putting less strain on the tender mouths of the haddock as they were being brought to the surface and boated.

When setting under sail, after the last dory had been dropped off the skipper and cook would ease the schooner down to leeward, keeping a sharp eye out, and in due course pick up the dories as they finished their sets. With the gang back and on board mugging up and the dories in tow, the vessel tacked back and forth, killing time until the fish were presumed to have taken the hooks if they were going to, when the dories were again dropped off at the weather buoys. Once more the Old Man would coast her down to leeward, jogging and picking up the loaded dories when the mates raised an oar to signal that the trawl was all aboard or that the boat was loaded, with more to haul yet.

For two men, skipper and cook, to shoot an eighty-foot schooner of seventy tons alongside a dory half down to its gunwales with fish, gear and oilskinned dorymates, in a stiff breeze and a sloppy sea, so neatly that she would creep almost to a stop beside the bobbing craft and pause long enough for cook to catch the painter, was a nice feat of seamanship. Some could carry it off without breaking an egg (not that they had one to spare) between the one and the other. And some couldn't, or on occasion didn't.

Such was a certain Gloucester captain, preferring anonymity, who wrote of approaching one of his dories in the summer of 1879, ranging farther ahead than he figured and striking it a glancing blow. It was supposed the three dorymen were thrown into the water, but as he was ordering another dory over and to the rescue, two of his victims came climbing aboard over the bow, having grabbed the bowsprit rigging. The third was found standing dripping wet in the unhurt dory, blood streaming down his face where the bow of the schooner had come down on his head and knocked him overboard. He had climbed back in. "I'm the proper lad to go haddocking," he laughed to his mates. "It don't bother me much to be run down!"

Aboard the fresh halibuters, once the dories were home and the men had jackassed the massive fish up over the rail, dressing proceeded with surgical efficiency in spite of a horrible roll and playfully boarding seas that had the crew up to their knees. Hence oilskins and boots. Working in gangs, they gutted and blooded the halibut. The "scrubber," distant relation to the surgeon's helper ashore, swept out the guts with his special broom and pails of water and hove the fish down the hatch into the icehouse, where one chilled crewman pounded the compacted ice loose with a mallet while his chilled mates hoisted the halibut onto the growing pile in the pen and covered it with crushed ice, ready for the next.

Contrarywise, the haddockers — making short, fast trips to market — were more casual dressers. Without the convenience of tables or tubs, they dressed the haddock directly in the pens where the fish lay, tossing the liver and roe into barrels nearby; then they washed them and just left them there if they were close to port in winter, or threw them below for icing. When the fishing was lively, the haddockers would be at it all day, dressing all evening and baiting most of the night until time to set out again in the morning.

Most meticulous were the salt bankers. Working at one of the splitting tables along the rail, the "header" ripped open the belly of the codfish, flipped the head overboard for the gulls and passed the fish to the "gutter," who removed and dropped the liver in a basket, hove the gurry over the rail and handed the carcass to the "splitter." The splitter deftly cut out the backbone and dropped the codfish, now spread-eagled, so to speak, into the washtub, where it was cleaned by the "idler" and tossed down the hatch. Down in the fish hold the "salters" scooped and slewered just the right dose of salt across the now-split remains and laid them up in the kenches, which were periodically repacked as they shrank and settled from the action of the salt, to the extent, indeed, of requiring that the bilges of the vessel be regularly pumped out.

The hazards of dory-trawling can be imagined. Fog and sudden squalls of wind, rain, snow, sleet or all four at once would descend on the water or sweep across it almost without warning, leaving the men no chance to row back to the safety of their schooner, nor even sight or sound of her. No compass either, often as not.

One who did imagine the doryman's lot, and with powerful reality, was Winslow Homer, whose ominous painting *The Fog Warning* portrays a lone Gloucester fisherman with a couple of halibut in the stern, pulling for his distant schooner as a foreboding fog creeps across the horizon. *Lost on the Grand Banks* pictures the dory wallowing in the trough as the dorymates, abandoning their oars, peer fearfully over the gunwale at an empty sea. Homer loved Gloucester and depicted her fishermen as no one else has, before or since.

Aboard his anchored schooner, his dories out, the worried skipper blew his whistle or cranked away at his Lothrop patented horn, clanged his bell, sent off flares, lit torches, even blasted off a swivel gun to reveal his position, and many the dory listened its way home in that dripping, stifling, utterly confusing thick-o'-fog that cannot be conceived truly by one who has not been engulfed in it at sea. And many didn't, if they were not directly to leeward, for the lightest breeze could blow sound away like a will-o'-the-wisp. Fog and snow obliterated the brightest lantern hung in the highest rigging, the fieriest rocket. Nor could skipper and cook, helpless to weigh anchor by themselves in a heavy squall or any other, sail off to the rescue. Fortunate were the dorymen who chanced to be directly downwind when storm and sea were too much to row against, for there was a chance then for those on board to let the wind carry an empty dory, if they had one, down to the fellows in trouble on a mile or more of line, if they had it and it held, and haul them back.

Many a dory, caught in a squall or boarded by a freak sea, flipped on the spot, unseen and unheard. It was a thousand-to-one shot that the lad who hung on by the becket from the dory plug in the bottom would be spotted before he gave up, exhausted and frozen, and sank beneath the wave. Too often his sea boots were the fisherman's friends, once he was in the drink, as few Gloucestermen bothered to learn to swim, abiding by the fatalistic injunction that it's better to get it over with fast.

The separation from the schooner, the wandering, the suffering, the starvation during those seventy or eighty years of dory-trawling were taken for granted by Gloucester with the resignation of the home front in war-time. There was no great stir when in the spring of 1886 four men in two dories went astray from the *Cecil H. Low* for some seven days before the two survivors were picked up, telling stories of attempted cannibalism.

There was no more than streetcorner talk about the two who went adrift from the *Solomon Poole* on the Grand Bank in July of 1882. After eight days without food and with little water, if any, they were taken up by a brig that fed them hard tack all the way to Brazil, whence they arrived back in Gloucester in September. Turning the trick, a doryman astray from the *Matthew S. Greer* in May 1919 rowed eighty miles into Halifax in two days and nights without food and arrived in Boston in time to greet the *Greer* at the dock when she sailed in with her flag at half-mast.

The sea was not always to blame. Two men from the *Dora A. Lawson* were setting their trawl on the Grand Bank on August 26, 1894, when a Spanish barque hove to nearby and asked for fish. They boarded her and swapped their entire catch for gin. Shortly after the barque sailed off, another dory crew, noticing the advancing befuddlement of their mates, advised them to get back aboard the *Lawson* and offered to finish setting for them. They refused. Later their dory was missing, and it was obvious they got so drunk they capsized and drowned.

And then there were the filthy hooks that snagged and had to be dug out of dirty flesh with dirty knives, or pulled out, or backed out, an open invitation to blood poisoning. Two dorymen from the *Grace L. Fears* were dumped into the sea when caught by a whopper of a wave one November day in 1880 while hauling their trawl. One hauled himself back aboard, tied the trawl to the bow and began bailing furiously. Meanwhile his mate had been carried down by the weight of his boots and oilskins when he chanced to tangle with the trawl. Instinctively, he pulled himself up by the line, hand over hand, only to snag a hook in a finger, clear to the bone. Reaching up with his free hand, he tore the hook from the flesh. Just as he broke the surface another hook grabbed a trouser leg. Lungs bursting, he seized the dory gunwale and in one desperate lunge ripped the hook from the fabric and flopped senseless into the bottom. When he came to, he insisted that they finish hauling the trawl.

Or caught in the ice floes of the subarctic. Run down in the fog by an unseeing steamer, as the *Mary P. Mesquita* was. Downed by the dread erysipelas, St. Anthony's fire, a horrible gangrenous infection of the hands, arms and face from handling fish in unsanitary conditions. Crippled for life by frostbite. An infinite variety of accidents available without a moment's notice aboard the vessel. These (and let us not forget pneumonia) were among the nasty host of afflictions and woes for which the fisherman was awarded no compensation except his life, if that.

Frostbite. The greatest of the dorymen, the hero of the nautical world in his day, was Howard Blackburn, a giant figure in the most gripping of Gloucester's uncounted sagas of death and survival at sea.

Fresh-halibuting in January of 1883, the young Nova Scotia native and his dorymate from Newfoundland, Tom Welch, were separated from the *Grace L. Fears* in a bitterly cold, blinding snowstorm on Burgeo Bank off the Newfoundland east coast. Welch weakened, gave up and froze to death. Blackburn kept bailing and pounding ice to keep the dory from foundering.

When his mittens were accidentally bailed overboard, Blackburn realized instantly that his bare hands would soon freeze and curled them around the oar handles so they would stiffen in the shape of his grasp.

The gale passed. With the frozen corpse of the man he was determined to take to a decent burial, Blackburn rowed sixty miles into the snowbound and virtually deserted Newfoundland coast without food or water in a five-day ordeal that ground the congealed flesh from his hands until he was pulling on the oars with his bones.

The Lishman family, near starving themselves, found him and nursed him back to life. In the spring Blackburn returned to Gloucester and acclaim, minus all his fingers, half of each thumb and most of his toes. For years he ran a famous saloon on the Gloucester waterfront, and they came from everywhere to gawk at him and buy a beer just to watch him pick up the dime from the bar.

Ever restless, Howard organized a Klondike gold expedition in 1897. In 1899 he pulled off the almost unbelievable feat of sailing his thirty-foot gaff-rigged sloop *Great Western* to England, single-handed and fingerless. Then he did it again, to Portugal in 1901 in the twenty-five-footer *Great Republic*. A third try for a transatlantic round trip in a sailing dory failed. Blackburn had a few more adventures and misadventures and died in bed in 1932 at the age of seventy-three, a legend in his own time.

None of his dorymates in the larger sense fared as Howard Blackburn did, or were endowed with his combination of strength, will, luck and dramatic flair.

Small enough were the expectations, and rarely celebrated were the labors and sacrifices of the Gloucestermen tending their trawls three hundred miles from land. They earned commonplace obituaries, so commonplace was the occasion, in the *Cape Ann Advertiser*:

Sch. *Gatherer* arrived home from a halibuting trip on Sunday and reports speaking on Grand Bank sch. *Mary F. Chisholm* of this port with loss of two of her crew, Angus McIsaac and Martin Flaherty, while visiting their trawls.

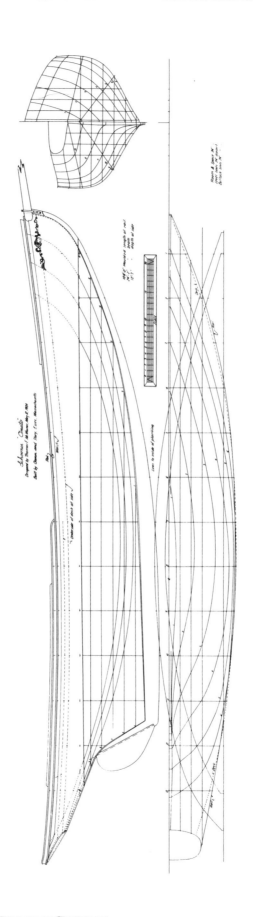

Ornato, 1904

DOWN TO THE SEA

Bound fishing, the Gloucester schooner *Onato* pushes along around 1905. *Onato* was a medium-large "Indian Header" designed by Tom McManus and built in 1904 by Oxner and Story at Essex. She was 106 feet long, one of several of an advanced, round-bowed type from the Boston designer's board, all given Indian names. And fast for her size, frequently logged at thirteen knots. One of *Onato*'s crew, Chester Morrissey, a Nova Scotia native of about eighteen, brought along a cheap box camera with which he snapped these rare photographs of a working Gloucesterman at sea. The camera never let him down, he claimed, even after it fell overboard once. After his career as skipper of dory trawlers, draggers and merchantmen, Captain Morrissey retired to Gloucester and loaned the author a batch of his ancient *Onato* negatives. He died in 1978 at ninety. (Chester L. Morrissey)

🐦 *1.* Helmsman's lot when his watch comes round on a wet and bone-chilling day leaves no recourse but to button up and batten down with oilskins — oiled cloth jacket and trousers, oiled sou'wester hat, mittens, boots, and a thick inside lining of resignation. The cold, foggy weather on the more distant banks didn't vary much with the seasons; "nine months winter and three months late in the fall," as the fishermen put it. (Chester L. Morrissey)

🐦 *2. Onato* surges onward through roistering seas, enough to test the stability of the strongest stomach. (Chester L. Morrissey)

84

3

3, 4. Early to rise makes a man healthy if not wealthy, the wisdom of it being that the early ones catch the fish aboard the big auxiliary schooner *Corinthian*, built for Gorton-Pew Fisheries of Gloucester by John F. James and Son at Essex in 1917. Chow is on the forecastle table just aft of the foremast, and Kit Hines and John Dahl dig in while a mate digs out. Up on deck, on the other hand, all is not so cozy. Two of a series of documentary photographs of a *Corinthian* trip commissioned by Gorton-Pew in the mid-1930s. (Edwin H. Cooper, Thomas Collection)

4

1. Baiting up by the mainmast of the *Corinthian* in a snow squall. What a way to make a living. (Edwin H. Cooper, Thomas Collection)

2. Hard was the lot of the Gloucester haddocker in the old times, up most of the night in the fish hold baiting trawls for the dawn sets. A rare view, rendered a hundred years ago, of the solemn proceedings. (Goode's *Fisheries*)

3. The hurdy-gurdy for hauling trawls, extra-heavy with halibut, one hoped, from the deep water was clamped on the bow gunwales. The smaller trawl roller was used generally in shoaler water and simply dropped in a hole in the rail. (Goode's *Fisheries*)

2

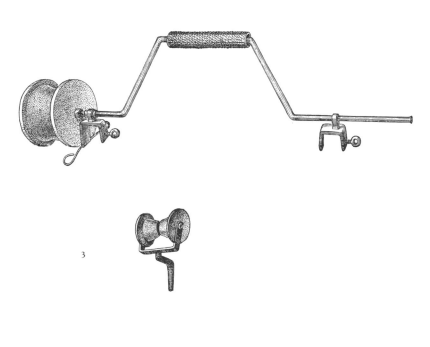

3

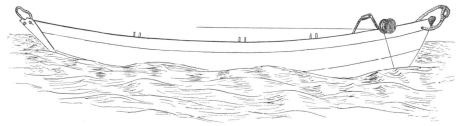

2

1. Out of the nest swings a dory from another large Gorton-Pew auxiliary schooner out of Gloucester, *Killarney*, built at Essex by Arthur D. Story in 1917. One is already overboard as two of the crew haul away on the forward tackle to the next. Trawl tubs await on deck. Bailing buckets and fog horns hang outside the bows of the dories so they will nest snugly. The two hauling are wearing "Cape Ann hats," oiled cloth like the sou'wester but having a narrow, even brim for use in lighter weather; the brim of the traditional sou'wester was longer in back to overlap the jacket collar and keep water from running down the wearer's neck. Locally manufactured oil clothes had the reputation of being the best in the world. A suit a hundred years ago cost about $3.50. Because oilskins stiffened and cracked in real cold weather, rubberized suits were often preferred by those who could afford them at $10. (Al Barnes, The Mariners' Museum)

2. Ready to sail and set, dories are cast off astern of the jogging schooner. (Albert Cook Church, The Whaling Museum)

1

1. Dorymates on a lonely, leaden sea . . . from the *Corinthian*. (Edwin H. Cooper, Thomas Collection)

2. The mark buoy and a near-doryload of large halibut have been hauled as the dorymates work their way upwind. Captain Collins used this sketch to illustrate his contemporary account of Howard Blackburn's saga, *Fearful Experience of a Gloucester Halibut Fisherman, Astray in a Dory in a Gale off the Newfoundland Coast in Midwinter*, published in 1884. (Goode's *Fisheries*)

3. The young Howard Blackburn, recently home in Gloucester from his ordeal. With time, he grew less loath to show his stumps of fingers, and even enjoyed palming a dime from the bar of his famous saloon, which never failed to mystify transient beer drinkers. (Author's Collection)

90

2

3

1

2

92

3

1. Back alongside *Onato,* the dorymen pitch up their contribution to the deepening deck-load. Dressing knives are at the ready on the side of the cabin trunk, and so is the ship's dog, who sniffs an ocean-fresh meal. (Chester L. Morrisey)

2. Bound home for Gloucester, all hands aboard *Onato* enjoy a round of dogplay. (Chester L. Morrissey)

3. Jogging along under foresail in a sloppy sea, another big Gloucesterman keeping company with *Onato* for a while is snapped in a powerful photograph by Chet Morrissey with his box camera. The jib is triced part way up the jibstay, rather than along the bowsprit, to keep it out of the way of the plunges. A little too rough right now for fishing. (Chester L. Morrissey)

94

2

1. The old-time Georgesman *Otis P. Lord*, built at Gloucester in 1876, looks to be bound out around the turn of the century, though hardly in Bristol fashion. Dory is on deck to starboard, and various lines trail astern from the davits. The mainboom crutch hasn't yet been stowed, and the main topping lift, which apparently was used to hoist the boom clear of the crutch when the crew raised sail, remains too taut and creases the canvas aloft. The pennant halyard from the boom to the end of the main gaff needs to be eased too. The vertical strips on the main and foresails take the brunt of the chafe from the respective after shrouds when running free with the wind. The lower of the boards between the stern davits is the "reefing plank" on which the men stand while reefing the mainsail in a blow, using the higher to hang on to, more or less. (Ernest L. Blatchford, Thomas Collection)

2. Few are the photos of a Georgesman at sea, and here is a smasher, of the *Genesta*, built at Gloucester by John Bishop in 1904. It's November 1920. One of the crew scuttles away from a couple of inquisitive barrels of sea water. (C.R. Patterson, Peabody Museum of Salem)

1

2

1. Lazily adrift on Georges Bank, sails limp and sheets slack, *Genesta* rides a slow swell while her crew ply their lines at the leeward rail. (Peabody Museum of Salem)

2. Captain Dobson of *Genesta*, clad in his old-fashioned barvel, an oilcloth apron, displays the prey. Heavy lead sinkers are required to keep the hooks "tending bottom" against the infamous Georges current. (Peabody Museum of Salem)

3. At the starboard rail of a Georgesman in the 1880s, one burly Gloucesterman gaffs up a hefty codfish, his mate cuts out a tongue to add to his tally, the third tends his line against his "sojer." The catch is tossed in pens for dressing later. The old-timers claimed that if the decapitated body seemed alive after the header had handed it to the splitter, a blow on the separated head would finish the job. (Goode's *Fisheries*)

⌇ "February on Georges" is all photographer Church said, or needed to say, about this one taken early in the century. (Albert Cook Church, The Whaling Museum)

6. GEORGES

Early in February, on the arrival of their supply of bait, the Georges fleet fit away for their early trips . . . No class of vessels are better calculated for a battle with the storm-king, and no braver souls tread the deck, but the contest is an unequal one, and many a staunch craft and gallant crew go down in the conflict. In a single storm, on the night of Feb. 24, 1862, fifteen Gloucester vessels and one hundred and twenty men were lost, leaving seventy widows and one hundred and forty fatherless children to mourn for the loved ones who would return no more.

— *The Fisheries of Gloucester*, 1876

Winter was at its cruelest on the Georges, and Georges was at its cruelest in the winter.

Georges Bank lies about 125 miles east-southeast of Gloucester, a twenty-hour sail in a good breeze. Eighty-five hundred square miles of shoals in depths from two to fifty fathoms, a tide-torn, storm-ripped battleground of currents and, strangely, one of the world's great nurseries of fish.

Georges was first exploited in 1830 by Gloucestermen looking for halibut. They found them, and when they had fished out the big ones they were left with the cod, the endless cod. Georges remained the nigh exclusive fishing ground of the Gloucestermen almost to the present day, until the oil drillers came upon the scene to strike a fear into the hearts of the brave souls that no storm-king ever could. The more ironic that as price for its unpolluted bounty of 150 years, Georges Bank has taken more Gloucester fishermen and more Gloucester vessels than all the rest of the fisheries combined — surely a heavier toll than exacted by any other in the world.

At the crest of the wave a hundred years ago, or the bottom of the trough, about twelve hundred of the Gloucester fishing population were afflicted with the Georges death wish, in batches of eight to twelve, not large as crews ran in those days. Roughly a third were native Yankees, a third "Down-Homers" from down home in the Canadian Maritimes, and the rest mainly Portuguese, Swedes and Irish. It was most likely Captain Joseph W. Collins, himself of Celtic extraction, who delivered this anonymous profile of them in the Goode report:

The successful result of a trip to George's Bank for codfish is largely dependent upon the exertions of each individual; men are, therefore, required for that fishery in whose natures is combined hardihood, doggedness of purpose, and bravery. Owing to the fact that each man's success depends in a great part on his individual efforts, the Portuguese and Irish have a special fondness for this fishery, though many others engage in it.

Many of the best fishermen and most capable skippers follow the George's fishery; but, as a rule, the crews are considered intellectually inferior to those employed in the mackerel and halibut fisheries. The results obtained depending so much on the individual efforts of the men, a vessel may make a successful trip under the control of a skipper who would be totally incapable of commanding a halibut schooner or one employed in the Grand Bank cod fisheries.

Appalled as he was by the risks and the losses in the Georges fisheries, Collins elsewhere in his writings made it plain that under the circumstances anyone, skipper or crew, who went fishing there was a damn fool, albeit a brave one. And there was no braver fisherman than he.

Arriving on the easterly edge of the shoals, the Georgesman dropped his anchor and took up a berth within a long hail of his neighbor on the temptingly fatal notion, it would seem, that misery loves company. He then furled his canvas and set a patch of riding sail in place of his main.

The Georges tides run amok, first this way, then that, meeting themselves head-on in all manner of queer eddies, spouts and falls. As a rule the men plied their lines by day, and when possible on a slack tide, for when the current was running at full tilt, perhaps two knots, it would lift the hooks clear off the bottom, sinker and all, unless nearly the entire nine hundred feet of line was let out.

The long Georges handline of heavy steam-tarred cotton, coiled in its tub at the ready, terminated in an eight- or nine-pound cylindrical lead sinker from the lower end of which angled off a "horse," a wooden or metal arm that suspended a double line down to a fifteen-inch crosspiece like a trapeze bar, known quaintly as a "sling-ding." To the ends of the sling-ding were tied nine-foot lines, "snoods," a pair of them ending with shorter ganging lines, to each of which was knotted a hook. A Georgesman carried as many as twenty thousand frozen herring on a two- or three-week winter trip. The men slivered these as they needed them, cutting each sliver into half a dozen little chunks per hook.

When fishing, the skipper put his helm down so his vessel would sheer across the tide. The men worked to leeward with the current, keeping their lines from entangling by plying them against "sojers," wooden pins driven with military precision every four feet or so into fishing rails nailed on top of the regular cap rails aft of the fore and main rigging, a peculiarity of the Georgesmen. Every now and again, muttering and shaking their heads with frustration, they had to haul back and fish over the opposite rail when the tide veered unexpectedly under the schooner, never, of course, in cooperation with the wind.

An old hand paid out his line rapidly until he felt the lead sound the bottom, when he let the current raise it slightly, hauled in a little, sounded again, thus "tending the bottom" until he had a couple hooked, and then hauled back, maybe taking half an hour to wrestle a pair of big ones to the surface and gaff them aboard.

The codfish were worked off the hooks, their tongues cut out for keeping tally, and the gangings replaced with a pair baited in the meanwhile, and back over with the lead. This way, a high-line fisherman on his best day might boat nearly two hundred fish, and a lucky crew as much as thirty thousand pounds in the round, eviscerated. If he chanced upon a halibut, each man cut his own distinctive mark in it for counting in his favor.

The fish were there all right, but what a deadly game! The best fishing was in the worst place, naturally, the east and southeast rim of the shoals in two to twelve fathoms, where the waves broke in rough weather. This was one hell of a lee in an easterly storm. Chided Goode's government survey, again probably in the words of Captain Collins:

The principal cause of disaster is the reckless daring of the fishermen, who persist in remaining at anchor in close proximity to other vessels even when they see the gale is coming, and, by removing their anchorage a short distance, they might greatly lessen the risks of disaster. They are led to remain in the same position, and to take resulting risks, both from the fear of losing an opportunity of securing a fare of fish, and from the dislike to the appearance of timidity.

Brave souls all right, but damn fools. No wonder Collins steered clear of the Georges. All this bravado multiplied when the visibility was reduced to next to nothing by thick snow, and skippers obstinately refused — perfectly understandably — to wield the ax until the last second because their anchor cables were not insurable. Furthermore, halyards, sheets and sails were often as not so stiff and immobilized with ice and snow as to make it quite impossible to get up sail in an emergency.

Such a fix on Georges in the late 1870s was described by Walter Hill. It was February; they had a berth on the southeast shoals among several other Gloucestermen and had caught and dressed a few fish when it came on to blow from the dread northeast and to snow as bitingly as hail so that a man could hardly keep his face to it on lookout.

Night fell, a driving snow, a howling gale. A sudden wild sea surfed aboard and sent the watch climbing up the foremast to avoid being swept overboard, and then a hell of a yell from him that brought all hands rushing up on deck.

The skipper has already placed himself at the cable, with a sharp axe, and every eye is straining into the gloom to distinguish the fatal light — for light it is — surely approaching! There is hope yet that the coming craft may drift across our bows without striking us, for the tide is setting over that way somewhat. Yonder she emerges from the gloom, and we can distinguish the dim outline of her spars and hull. It seems as if nothing short of a miracle can prevent the danger from culminating. The skipper has twice lifted his axe to strike the severing blow from the cable, but the remembrance of the vessels to leeward of us causes him to hesitate. But for this we should doubtless have cut at the first alarm.

Now she rises on the crest of a sea, right ahead of us, and five seconds more will tell the tale. The suspense which thrills every breast suspends respiration; almost stops circulation. The tongue is powerless, and all the faculties are concentrated in the eyes. Every gaze is riveted on the vessel as she rises, more on the bow this time, and every man draws a great breath of relief, for we know that the danger is past!

She is now abreast of us, but going away slowly on the starboard quarter. So near is she that we feel her cable running up across our own, but we know from its buoyancy that there is no anchor on the end of it, so we have no fear of its hooking hold of us. Away into the gloom, out of sight, drifts the fated vessel, the crew unconscious of the new perils so near at hand, to leeward. The drift she was making when we lost sight of her would take her very, *very* near the vessel whose bearings we took on the starboard quarter before the storm set in. God help the poor fellows! To be adrift on Georges Bank at such a time, among a fleet of vessels, is a danger only to be realized by those who have been through some experience of the kind.

Is it by chance that the snow shortly after this suddenly ceases? The cessation is of but short duration, but as it clears to leeward all eyes are searching for the lights, and soon one is descried as it rises on the sea. We try to see the other — we know there must be two in that direction. The next sea reveals to all that there *are* two lights there, TOGETHER! A loud and horrified cry announces this discovery, and then every man seems frozen to a statue. The terrible interest centered in those entangled lights seems to suspend every sense but that of sight, which it intensifies.

This scene has scarcely become distinct, when like a vision it fades away. The snow falls again, and the lights disappear, whether behind the curtain of snow, or whether they sink into the embrace of the furious giant who was yesterday so softly enchanting us, we are in doubt. But of the end of the encounter there is, alas! no room even for doubt.

The rendezvous so chillingly described by Walter Hill occurred in fact on the eve of February 20, 1879. At four that afternoon the wind approached hurricane strength from the east, with thick snow and bitter cold. Most of the fleet of sixty Georgesmen was anchored about forty miles upwind of the southeast shoals. One week later twenty-four of the survivors had limped back to Gloucester with the news of how only the slow hauling of the wind to the north-northwest had saved them and, they prayed, a few others from being carried down on the main body of the fleet and then onto the shoals to almost certain destruction. After two more weeks of not another word, the *Cape Ann Advertiser* cried out:

A CLOUD OF SORROW

hangs over our city. Fourteen of the fishing fleet with their precious lives remain unaccounted for since the gale of February 20th. There are anxious hearts of wives, mothers, children, brothers and sisters, waiting for news of the safe return of the vessels which contain their loved ones. Eyes are watching for the return of the absent Georgesmen; hope is revived every morning, that ere the day closes it may bring home the overdue fishermen. There are sad forebodings as the hours glide by, which only God and the aching hearts will ever know of; there are prayers going up to Heaven in behalf of the absent men, and sympathetic hearts go out in tenderness toward those whose fears cause the hours to go by on leaden wings.

It is terrible! The very thought of the probable loss which o'ershadows this community is well-nigh overwhelming, and it is the theme on every tongue; the all-engrossing thought of our people.

Men knocked about like candlepins, decks swept of bulwarks, fish pens, windlasses, hatches, gear and dories. Dismasted, spars and sails and anchors and cable gone by the board. The crew of the schooner *Pioneer* told of losing their anchor and lurching off adrift, "and before the cable could be got in, a sea broke over the stern, smashing boat, bending davits, and burst into the riding sail, tearing it to ribbons."

The veteran skipper of another survivor declared that the twentieth of February, 1879, was the worst storm he'd ever been through. "The wind blew fearfully and its roaring through the rigging resembled the noise produced by a train of cars in crossing a bridge, while the snow was so thick that for more than 12 hours one could not see forty feet from the vessel."

Adrift at the worst of it, the crew of the *Jamestown* "saw a light from another schooner a short distance astern. This troubled them more than the gale or the bitter cold, for full well they knew if a collision took place, there would be two vessels of the fleet which would never return to port. They drifted by her so near that they could see the men on deck with their torches, and with thankful hearts went on their way and passed through the gale in safety."

Another schooner, caught farther to the eastward, had her dory swept away and her foresail shredded, and drifted before the storm under bare poles for two hundred miles before they dared make sail for Gloucester.

Three weeks dragged by and only one of the missing vessels had arrived home. All realistic hope had to be abandoned. Without doubt, thirteen Georgesmen had disappeared beneath the waves with 143 men aboard, in the most awful single disaster in the history of the American fisheries. Before the year 1879 was out, the count would be twenty-nine Gloucester schooners and 249 men, by far the most of them gone down with their vessels.

Fishermen had no life insurance. There was no welfare. A grim George Procter and his *Cape Ann Advertiser* did what they could. "This winter fishing on Georges is, at best, a perilous occupation. There is none more so in the known world . . . Have it well understood that the catching of a trip of fish shall not be paramount to the safety of men's lives." The news went forth and help poured back from around the country, $28,216.72 in all, and food, clothing, coal and wood for fifty-six shattered families.

In the old Fort section down on the harbor the *Advertiser* found a new widow with six children, all sick, no food in the house. In another house there was no wood for the stove, no food in another, nothing but rags for clothing in another. Everywhere, despair.

The widow of one of the drowned skippers spoke for all:

"It was many weeks ere I could make up my mind that my husband would not come again. I have watched the vessels from my window, praying for God to bring him back. He did not want to go on the trip, but was over-persuaded by his crew, who were all first-class men, and wished to be earning. He seemed to have a warning that it would be a disastrous trip; but what could he do? He was in debt and wished to settle. I feel that it is all well with him in Heaven, and feeling assured of this, I shall strive my best to so live and bring up our children, that we shall meet him there.

"But I do miss him so much — it seems as if he must enter that door. No one can tell how lonely I am, but thank God I can pray, and this gives me strength to believe that the God of the widow and fatherless will not forsake me."

7. MEN AND MASTERS

Had the Grand Bank been infested with seagoing tribes of hostile redskins — had halibut thieves and dory rustlers lurked in the fogs of Georges — the Gloucester fisherman, his trusty gobstick and his beloved schooner might have been immortalized with about the same mix of fact and fancy as the cowboy and the Wild West. The average doryman, with the astonishing exception of Howard Blackburn, had about as much flair for folk heroism as the average cowpoke; life was a little more grim out there on Burgeo Bank, that's all.

Then too, the territorial combat so necessary to the western didn't seem quite so vital on the eastern rim of Sable, with nothing to be surveyed but 360 degrees of water, nor were the members of the weaker sex so essential to the cast (or crew) as objects of rivalry, for there were none. Deprived of these important ingredients of romance, the old-time fisherman as a type of the rugged American individualist emerged at worst in the role of bewhiskered caricature and at best as a vaguely disturbing anonymity.

Not all by coincidence, the truest and cruelest drama that was the real essence of the Gloucester way of life and death played itself out before an audience of late Victorian romantics. The fishermen were so rough and innocent, their schooners so staunchly vulnerable. Here was melodrama in the raw, unwritten though rehearsed for two hundred and fifty years: the sea, the wind, the man-made vessel, the undaunted spirit, the lowly prey, the exploitation, foreclosure by the fate of fates, tempests, fogs, sudden disaster in the night, a watery grave, the thin-lipped widow, the orphaned child.

And it was all too true — the reverse of the Victorian coin.

Not out of this Gloucester business but around it poured forth much bad verse ("Loving and longing and true, Gilding her idol of clay / Bride, when the boat comes in; Widow, it sails away" — by the summer lady of Eastern Point, Elizabeth Stuart Phelps), and very rarely some of the best ("Where is there an end of them, the fishermen sailing / Into the wind's tail, where the fog cowers?" — from *The Dry Salvages* by the summer boy of Eastern Point, T. S. Eliot).

Rudyard Kipling, whose forte was supposed to be India and Empire, visited Gloucester a couple of summers, took a quick trip on a schooner that turned his stomach and wrote the finest fishing narrative ever, his novel *Captains Courageous*, first published serially in 1896.

The same year James Brendan Connolly, son of seagoing Aran Islanders who had immigrated to South Boston, quit Harvard and won the hop, step and jump race in Athens, the first gold medalist in the first Olympic Games in fifteen hundred years. Connolly took up journalism, discovered Gloucester, did some serious sailing on the schooners and followed through on Kipling's accurate though heavily dialected and slightly patronizing novel with a string of rollicking, zestful yarns and short stories. Jim Connolly's tales exalted the stout hearts of the fishermen (with a happily Celtic bias, it must be admitted), personalized and glorified the vessels and captured eloquently the excitement of plowing along through the crested seas with every stitch of canvas aloft, every sheet straining, every pulse pounding and the decks awash to the wheelhouse.

Many the feature writer discovered and rediscovered the glamour of tall ships a'sailing and the pungent romance of busy wharves and quaint streets, but it was Kipling and Connolly, the Anglophile and the Anglophobe, who really invented the rest of the world's image of Gloucester, an image that with time and the passing of sail ossified into stereotype.

An unpopular demurrer to all this well-written macho of the sea was delivered by the widely read novelist of conviction and sentiment, the redoubtable and humorless Miss Phelps. The lady and the fishermen did not mix. First, she aroused their blood pressure by exerting her considerable influence in high places to have the warning whistling buoy off Eastern Point removed for three summers in the 1880s because its groans made her nervous.

Inspired by the unhappy consequences of a drunken murder perpetrated down the road from her summer cottage, Phelps had already leaped into the local temperance movement of 1876. She was still at it twenty years later, even as Kipling's great adventure story was issuing forth, with a tongue-lashing for the fishermen and their dissolute way of life in a magazine article one reader complained gave strangers the impression that "without exception [the men] are indeed a depraved lot of mortals, who live in wooden huts by the sea where they are principally engaged in quenching their alcoholic thirst and beating poor defenceless women until they are black and blue."

Where her adopted summer roost was concerned, Elizabeth Phelps displayed characteristic Victorian myopia, concentrating on the consequences of drunkenness, with short shrift for its causes and possibly even provocations. The temperance reform of 1876 rode in on one of those periodic crests of genteel moral revulsion that swept over Gloucester, culminating in the tidal wave of Prohibition some forty-three years later. One of the effects was a reduction in the number of publicly acknowledged saloons along the waterfront from twenty-six to fifteen. Another was a general agreement among the owners to ban liquor from the vessels, including even the medicine chest. The effect on the fancy houses is unrecorded.

Down at the Phoenix Billiard Parlor and Restaurant at the head of Duncan Street, where "fishermen and landsmen will find this a cozy retreat to while away an evening," the old port enjoyed the reputation as among the toughest on the Atlantic, engaged in the hardest of all maritime pursuits. The livelihood of nearly everyone in the city depended on fishing in some way, and fishermen dominated an industry so profligate of them that it had to seek elsewhere to keep its ranks filled.

Thus Gloucester was a mecca for thousands of the footloose, put on its mettle to provide attractions for strangers, many of them a rough lot, who were not customarily welcomed in the homes of the good people on whose behalf they plied their lines. In a well-intentioned if moralistic stab at sizing up the Gloucestermen of the day, the Goode Commission report of a hundred years ago (Captain Collins the probable author) had this to say:

In large ports, like Gloucester, whither flock the discontented, the disgraced, and the ne'er-do-wells, as well as the most enterprising and ambitious of the young men from the whole coast, there is, of course, less attention paid to the question of morals than in rural communities, and the general moral tone of the fishing classes is below the average for the whole coast . . . There are, of course, depraved men among the fishermen whose vicious instincts are increased by the irregular character of their occupation, but a large majority of the fishermen, even of Gloucester, are pure in their morals.

Drunkenness, the writer stated earnestly, "is not a vice to which fishermen are addicted." The problems arise when the vessels put in for supplies and bait to remote ports such as along the Newfoundland coast, where liquor can be had (such as the Newfie version of rum, which was, Lord help us, in excess of 140 proof).

Either the connection was not made — or far worse, if made, it was dismissed — between the rise in intoxication among the fishermen that brought on the temperance reform of 1876 and the fact that the previous year 123 men and sixteen schooners had been lost out of Gloucester, and that 877 men and 129 schooners had not returned between 1870 and 1874. The year the dries triumphantly closed down two out of every five resorts for alcoholic solace and backbone-stiffening, 1876, the body count was 212 men and twenty-seven vessels.

During the entire Civil War Gloucester lost thirty-six men in battle.

Fearfulness served the ends of neither fisherman nor soldier. "Fishermen

107

are not as a rule given to forebodings of ill," declared the Goode Report. "They always go to sea with brave hearts, the idea that they may never return to port seldom being allowed consideration, no matter how many of their comrades have been lost within a few days."

Perhaps.

Howard Blackburn's ordeal of 1883, his triumph and his return bouts with his old enemy epitomized to a fascinated generation the theme of man against the sea, the essence of the Gloucester fisherman — the loner, after all, out there in a dory.

The precedent for the great Blackburnian single-handed crossings of the Atlantic had been staked out twenty-three years before he sailed to England in *Great Western* by another doryman, Alfred Johnsen, who set forth in a sailing dory from Gloucester on a dare to celebrate the Centennial of 1876 and reached the coast of Wales fifty-eight days later in the first such lone passage in recorded history.

Blackburn's 1901 record time of thirty-nine days in *Great Republic* stood for thirty-eight years. With that kind of tradition, Gloucester was just naturally the favored port of departure for all kinds of men in all kinds of small boats assaying the Western Ocean. The charisma of the port and the almost mystical tradition persisted. In the summer of 1980, at the age of sixty-five, Philip S. Weld of Gloucester, retired publisher of the *Gloucester Times*, won the Observer Single-handed Transatlantic Race in his fifty-one-foot sailing trimaran *Moxie*. His time of eighteen days from England to Newport was a new record for the crossing, in the mold of his predecessors.

Does it take one kind of courage to accept fate, another to tempt it? One to serve, another to command?

The conditions under which the fishermen of Gloucester entrusted their lives and their livelihoods to their captains and their vessels, and most generally still do, were governed by a unique and unspoken order of democracy.

The profits of the trip, if any, were shared among the men, the captain and the owners. Command and decision while at sea were the skipper's by common acquiescence. He alone had the responsibility for the management and safety of his schooner and his crew and for the success of the trip. But his men no more than consented to his authority; in case of accident they chose one of their own to take over, for there was by tradition no mate, no second in command.

The men dressed as they liked, worshiped or not as they liked and talked as they liked — meaning, as the government's God-fearing observer rebuked in 1887, that profanity was notorious aboard the schooners of Gloucester. "A few of the masters are opposed to the practice and endeavor to restrain it, but ordinarily no effort is made in this direction. Almost as common is the use of vulgar and indecent words."

The fishing captain shared his cabin with his men, and ate with them. He tried to make orders sound like requests. His power to compel the dissatisfied to stay on board was limited, and he had little recourse if a hand failed to show up at the start of a trip or jumped ship in the course of one. Not a few masters returned to Gloucester with broken trips, busts, because of mutinous conduct they couldn't handle, and even the most rugged of the lot thought twice before using his fists for fear of assault charges once back ashore.

The Gloucester skipper, wrote one who knew whereof he wrote in the Goode Report, probably Collins, "must be a natural leader, and generally gifted with superior intellect and tact, in order to get along with the crew, there being no special laws like those in the marine service, which give him authority over his men. In cases of insubordination he must have recourse to his physical strength. If he cannot sustain himself in this manner, his influence over the crew is gone."

Little wonder that so many Gloucester captains achieved legendary status as master mariners larger than life in their own lifetimes. An iron hand must wear a velvet glove "in a port like Gloucester, where the fishermen are of different nationalities and are often men who have been unable to hold their own in other ports on account of their notoriously bad characters."

Sometimes leadership, intellect and tact were not enough. There were trips when a string of bad luck took over, and the best skipper alive, with the skill of St. Peter and the patience of Job, could barely sustain himself. Such a poor trip — not a broker or a total bust, but an utter discouragement — was by no means uncommon. An indifferent fishing voyage, dutifully logged by a conscientious master, may reveal an unintended view of the conditions, the men and the tensions on a Gloucester schooner as they really were in the peak days of sail, not as they flowed from the novelist's pen.

There was a scarcity of hands on the waterfront in the spring of 1891, and Captain Eben Macauley, age forty, on May 14 cleared the John F. Wonson Company wharf in East Gloucester in the Wonson schooner *Henry W. Longfellow* for a summer of salt fishing on the Grand Bank of Newfoundland. The *Longfellow*, a strong vessel of eighty-one tons, was built by Willard Burnham in Essex in 1883. Ballast had been taken out for this trip to make more room for salt. Shorthanded, Macauley figured to fill out his crew down along the coast of his native Nova Scotia. Along with his gear he had his log, bound in black oilcloth for protection against the weather.

Their passage was uneventful across the Gulf of Maine, by Cape Sable and along the Novie south shore to Liverpool, where Eben sent Ennis, the cook, and Whitman, a fellow Bluenose, ashore to recruit. They returned empty-handed, but in the meantime he had signed on a Frenchman, and farther along at Port Hawkesbury, John Purcell, Hugh McEachern and the

McDonalds — Dan, Malcolm and John — as hired hands at an average of $80 for the trip, as opposed to the regulars who were on shares. They were still in harbor when Alex Fraser came down with the measles, and Whitman with such a bad case of the grippe that the captain had to leave him ashore in the hospital with a $25 deposit on the bill.

The *Longfellow* took on ice and sailed through the long and narrow Strait of Canso between Nova Scotia proper and Cape Breton Island, into the Bay of St. Lawrence and up the Cape shore to Judique in search of bait. None there. Purcell, McEachern and the Frenchman were seasick. No bait at the Magdalen Islands. Crossed the Cabot Strait to Newfoundland. No bait at Bay St. George. None at Bay of Islands, where the natives said the herring hadn't spawned yet. Hung around for two days, and when the herring struck in, bought twenty-four barrels at a dollar each.

The gang baited up three tubs of trawl to a dory on the way, and the *Longfellow* reached the grounds on June 8. As if on signal, John McDonald, Purcell, John Bisher and McEachern broke out with the measles, and Fraser, who had been mending, took a notion to relapse. But the rest kept fishing until their bait and ice gave out. Eben stood in for shore and bought three doryloads of ice, but there was no bait to be had.

On June 17 they hove to off the French island of St. Pierre and sent in a dory. Again, no bait. Alex Fraser was feeling well enough to have a brawl with Charlie Nickerson, and on Eben's orders "the measles men took a dose of salts." On into Newfoundland's Placentia Bay, where they caught caplin by the tubful and made sail for the Grand Bank, wind southwest, heavy fog.

At the end of a week of dory-trawling on the Bank, the young captain noted in his log that Purcell was "used up from work" and in his bunk with cramps and a sore leg, and "I am sick myself today." On July 1 they spoke the schooner *Orpheus*; her crew claimed they had caught thirty tubs where they were anchored. Macauley's men made a quick set just beyond the outside buoys of the *Orpheus*, and when they hauled, not a hook had a fish on it.

Low on bait and out of ice on the Fourth of July, the skipper wrote: "Calm. Warm. No chance to get to land. Fate seems to work against me. Calm when I am making a passage and blowing when on the grounds. No observations today. All hands employed fixing trawls."

It came in thick again, almighty thick, and not a breath of wind, and the *Longfellow* drifted, carried on toward land by heavy, rolling seas. At six in the evening of the sixth they heard the groan of a distant whistling buoy. As the swell carried them closer, there was no doubt it was the whistler off Mistaken Point, and they were drifting toward the rocks of Newfoundland's Cape Race. Nothing to do but let go the anchor.

Early in the morning a little breeze sprang up. They hove in the hook, cleared the rocks and sailed into the baiting station of Cape Broyle, just

110

south of St. John's, where they took on fresh water, two tons of ice and six doryloads of caplin. During the night Purcell, the sickliest of the bunch, and Bisher ("dam scamp") jumped ship.

Macauley signed on two replacements, and in three days they were back at anchor on the Grand Bank in a fleet of twenty fogbound schooners that reported mighty poor fishing. The Gloucesterman cruised hither and yon without much luck. Fraser got into another fight, this time with Dan McDonald. They ran out of bait and ice, and back to Cape Broyle, where the gang went ashore and got drunk. With a supply of ice, caplin and squid, it was back again to the Grand Bank, where on July 26 Eben admitted to his log:

"Foggy. Sounded on Bank. Wind SE. Moderate. Bursted our staysail from slatting. Charles Nickerson sick and off duty. Thomas Rourke lazy and in his bunk. Some of the sharesmen very slow to do anything which shows bad example to our hired men. I done all I could to help my sharesmen, but I am getting discouraged myself. I am heartsick. William Verge is the best I got to take interest — good man. Betsie my cat is tomming. No tom cat on board."

The *Longfellow*'s luck was no better for the rest of July. One man or another was in his bunk sick every day. The only break in the grind of continual rowing, setting, hauling, dressing, baiting, with not much to show for it, was the bait run to Torbay, near St. John's, where they "had a good dance to Mrs. Goos," and McEachern and the unnamed Frenchman (probably unspellable) had a skinful.

Back to the Grand Bank, all fog and nasty. Macauley tried flying sets with no better luck. Tried jigging squid with the handlines for fresh bait. No better. The fore peak halyard parted, and they rove off a new one, and the jibboom sprung, and they fixed that.

August 15: "I dont know what to do. Men getting discouraged. Alex Fraser got the pants in bunk all day. William Verge went on board sch. Horace B. Parker. Got one bottle of gin and a Cape Ann Advertiser. The crowd drank the gin and I digested the paper."

Three days later all hands were put to work overhauling gear. John McDonald tripped and sprained his thumb. They ran into Bay Bulls for five tons of ice, but there was no bait. McEachern landed in the local lockup, drunk — an awful cut-up but one of his best, and Eben rowed in and paid the fine of $7.50. As much as the weather, bait was a chronic problem for the Bank fishermen. There was never enough room aboard the vessel because the salt took so much. Hard to keep it fresh, always running into the provincial ports for more, which took days and weeks out of the fishing and undercut the morale of all on board.

Captain Macauley wanted to try Flemish Cap, a shoal to the eastward, but the wind continued ahead into September. Frustration, frustration, even unto the day when "Lice struck in cabin."

At long last they sounded on Flemish Cap, and there were the codfish they'd been after for four months. Set after set, tub after tub, back and forth in the dories from dawn till dark, dressing on deck night after night under the lanterns until nine or ten o'clock.

Problems, problems for the skipper. McEachern had to be fished up once when the tackle parted and dumped his dory as it was being hoisted aboard. Next week the man had a fight with Rourke. The week after, a sea washed two tubs of trawl and an oar out of his dory, and he was lucky to get back to the schooner. Someone always ailing — sprained wrist, sore finger, stiff neck, John McDonald's sore mouth — "dont know what ails him," worried his captain.

It blew and it blew, winter in the air. The *Henry W. Longfellow* lay to anchor with trawls out for four days before the men could get to them — snow squalls — steamships lurching by, trailing thin smoke. On September 23 it moderated enough to put the dories over. The buoys marking twelve tubs of trawl were gone. The gang had hard work getting back aboard. A white squall carried away an empty dory trailing astern. Off to the southwest a schooner leaned for home, flag half-mast high.

Nearly five months out of Gloucester now, Eben Macauley wrote in the log on October 2: "Weather looks very bad. Cold for the time of year. No observations for a week." They took on some stores from the *William E. Morrissey*, bound back to Gloucester and Wonson's. Another brawl. Rourke hit his dorymate so hard the man broke the top strake of their dory when he went down.

The northers howled down on them, and the seas raged. At two in the morning on October 4 the *Longfellow* broke adrift. They hove in cable, thinking the anchor had fouled on something and broken out, but it was clear. They let it go again. She wouldn't fetch up, and they hove in the hook, made sail and fell off twenty miles before they could work back upwind to the buoys the next day and haul most, at least, of their trawls.

Blow, blow, blow as the *Longfellow* headed inshore again for bait. The mainboom tackle parted. They took in the mainsail. Jib blew out. Repaired and reset it. A crash of wind and driving rain. Took in the jib, reefed the foresail, set the stormsail. Wind moderated. Shook out the reef. Wind freshened. Reefed again. Moderated. Shook out the reef, set the mainsail, then the staysail. McEachern hurt by the foresheet. Stormed again. Took in staysail, mainsail and jib, reefed the foresail and set the stormsail. Wind hauled to the west and moderated. Shook out the reef. Set the mainsail, jib and staysail.

So it went, day and night for five days, and they made it into Bay Bulls. "No squid caught." Eben was gritting his teeth now. "Natives too lazy." Wolfe and Fraser rowed ashore, got roaring drunk and fighting. Skipper shut off liberty for four on board because Nickerson and Mal McDonald were not back for their watch. At seven p.m. "cook ashore against my orders." Nickerson staggered back aboard.

They jigged up a few tubs of squid, sailed down to Cape Broyle where four of the crowd got "drunk, very drunk," picked up their mail and off again for the grounds. Eben was *bound* to fill out the trip before going home.

Sounding, came to anchor on Artimon Bank between Misaine and Banquereau. Strong gale, with rain and hail. Set the stormsail.

"October 20. 4 a.m. Hove in cable. Calm. Very heavy sea running. Wind hauled to NNE. Squall parted cable at 5 a.m. Lost anchor, 40 fathoms cable. 6 a.m. bent on another anchor. Fetched her up at 7 a.m. Vessel half full of water. Started both pumps. Freed her at 9 a.m. Dont know what caused her to leak. She is as tight as a cup now at 6 p.m. and always was before — only that one time. Moderating at sundown. Baited three tubs to a dory. Too rough to set."

A week later, with calms enough for only three or four sets, Captain Macauley ordered the cable hove in for the last time and made sail for Nova Scotia. "No more fishing this trip."

Back at Port Hawkesbury he wired Wonson's for money to pay off the hired hands and was bottled up there by headwinds for six more days before it came in northwest, then easterly, sending them on their way.

At seven in the morning of November 7, 1891, the *Henry W. Longfellow* eased back alongside the Wonson wharf in Smith Cove, gone six months lacking a week. It took two days to unload 105,000 pounds of salt fish. The crew's share came to $150.05 a man for half a year's work. Eben's was probably about double.

Captain Macauley went skipper for John F. Wonson Company for three more years, when he quit the sea to work ashore for them. It was pretty generally accepted in those days that the hardest-working and most ambitious fishermen were about used up by the age of forty-five. Following a spell of poor health, Eben Macauley died of a heart attack at forty-nine.

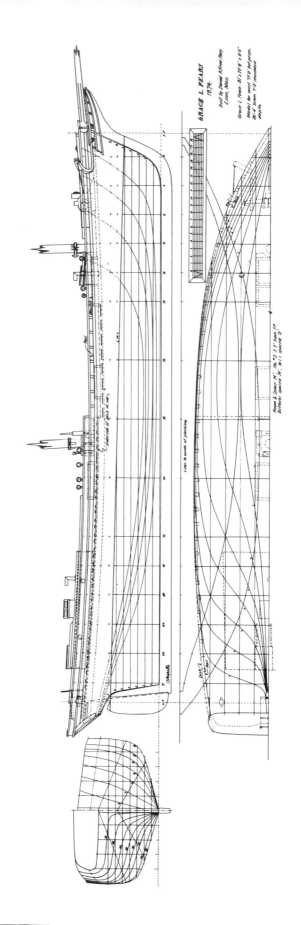

Grace L. Fears, 1874

1. Howard Blackburn was a portly Gloucester saloonkeeper of forty-one when he had Archibald Fenton build the twenty-five-foot sloop *Great Republic* in 1900 for his second single-handed crossing of the Atlantic, to Portugal the next year. Here he takes her for a trial spin in the harbor. After many adventures and numerous owners, *Great Republic* was brought home from Long Island in 1970 and restored by the Gloucester Historical Commission. The greatest Gloucesterman's gallant sloop awaits enshrinement in a waterfront park dedicated to his old friend, Captain Solomon Jacobs. (Sandy Bay Historical Society)

2. Twenty-six years have passed since Howard Blackburn's final and unsuccessful attempt to sail the Atlantic alone in the dory *America*. Now seventy, he sits at the wheel of his last boat, the sloop *Cruising Club*, after her launching at Gloucester in the summer of 1929. Blackburn built and named the thirty-two-footer in reciprocal honor of the Cruising Club of America, which had elected him a rare honorary member. *Cruising Club* was acquired in 1976 by the author, who sailed her on several Maine cruises before she was wrecked in a gale in Gloucester Harbor in 1979. (Adolph Kupsinel)

115

3

🕊 *1.* Some of the crew of the *Isabel* gather around for a good stir of the contents of what may be the liver butt. Clay pipes and diminutive derbies were de rigeur along the Gloucester waterfront in the 1880s. (The Smithsonian Institution)

🕊 *2.* Judging from the satisfactory appearance of the aproned cook at left, the grub on the *Lottie G. Merchant* is the finest kind, as they say on the waterfront. That's Captain Ben McGray, in the necktie of course. The *Merchant* was built in 1901, later was fitted with an auxiliary engine and fished for years in the William H. Jordan fleet. (Thomas Collection)

🕊 *3.* Splicing an anchor cable for a Gloucester fishing schooner in 1882 required three men and a large fid, the dark, conical, wooden implement protruding between the strands and used to separate them for insertion of the strands of the length being joined. A giant fid stands on the wharf to the right. Fish scales at the left. The lore decreed that a splice left in the hawse pipe when anchoring on the banks guaranteed mighty poor fishing until more cable was let out or hauled back. (U.S. Fish and Fisheries Commission, courtesy of The Smithsonian Institution)

117

1

🐦 *1, 2.* Captain Eben Macauley in his prime, and his pride and sometimes joy, the *Henry W. Longfellow*, at the John F. Wonson wharf on Smith's Cove in East Gloucester. A fare of salt fish is curing on Wonson's flakes. Across the cove are the wharves of Rocky Neck. (George O. Byard; the Alice Babson Collection, Cape Ann Historical Association)

🐦 *3.* Billy Corkum takes the helm, and she feels the master's touch. The imposing iron wheel and steering gears behind it in the wheelbox were made by the Gloucester machinists, A. P. Stoddart. By the turn of the century, scarcely a schooner in the fleet would venture beyond Eastern Point with anything but a Stoddart wheel turning the rudder post and at least one old hand, as pictured, to grasp it. (Thomas Collection)

2

1. The crew of the largest knockabout schooner out of Gloucester, the *Catherine*, owned and skippered by Captain Archie MacLeod, gather aft for the photographer in 1927. One of the last of the halibuters, *Catherine* was built by A.D. Story at Essex in 1915 — a big one, with tall spars, great sails, the longest forecastle in Gloucester (fifty-three feet), thirteen double dories and a crew to match. She piled up on Bald Rock Shoal off Canso, Nova Scotia, on New Year's Eve, 1933. All twenty-nine men got off in nine dories and made shore just before she took a lurch, the galley stove upset and *Catherine* burned to the water. (Thomas Collection)

2. Captain Jeffrey Thomas, in full regalia at the wheel of his first command out of Gloucester, the schooner *Cynthia*, in 1910. The Arichat, Nova Scotia, native, youngest of eight brothers, is thirty-five. *Cynthia* has seen plenty of hard fishing in the four years since she was built by John Bishop and Captain Jeff nearly lost her on her maiden trip when she ran aground in New York Harbor in the fog. Thomas had twelve more commands, most of them for Sylvanus Smith Company of Gloucester, before he died of a heart attack aboard his last, the schooner *Adventure*. They were dory-trawling eighty miles off Halifax on March 24, 1934, heavily iced up; the 260-pound skipper collapsed after chopping ice from the rigging. He was then fifty-nine. "A great sail carrier," his son Gordon called him, "and a tough man." (Thomas Collection)

121

1

2

122

3

🐚 *1.* Following the fish wherever they may lurk, the mackerel seiner *William M. Gaffney*, seineboat in tow, finds a light air off the Ten Pound Island lighthouse one day in the 1890s. The *Gaffney* was an extreme clipper built by David A. Story at Vincent's Cove in 1877. She carried an awesome spread of canvas, considerably reduced here since fore topmast, and therefore the fore topsail, fisherman's staysail and ballooner, are not set. A decade before this photograph, in the summer of 1880, Winslow Homer boarded in the keeper's cottage adjoining the lighthouse and painted scores of his most endearing Gloucester watercolors. The fully rigged and canvased builder's model of the *William M. Gaffney* is on display at the Sawyer Free Library in Gloucester, on loan from The Smithsonian Institution. (Martha Hale Harvey, Cape Ann Historical Association)

🕊 *2.* Before the purse seine revolutionized the fishery, every mackerel was caught and pulled up over the rail by hand — 153,892 barrels landed at Gloucester alone in the big year of 1863. At the starboard rail of this mackerel hooker in the midst of a vast fleet of them, the pair on the left are jigging with their baited lines, each hook embedded in lead, the "jig", the two in the middle with a deft backward motion are slatting off the hooked fish into their barrels; the fisherman on the right ladles out a scoopful of foul-smelling ground-up gurry called "chum" from the bait box outside the rail, his object being to "toll" or "chum" the mackerel toward the surface. (Goode's *Fisheries*)

🕊 *3.* Her seineboat at the ready, the *Irene and May* surges on in search of the schooling mackerel. Big anchors on her bows. A manila jib sheet chafes against the stay and sooner or later may part, hence the light chain. She was built by Oxner and Story at Essex in 1901. (Thomas Collection)

123

3

1. Skipper smells mackerel and orders the seineboat over. The schooner is *Pinta* of Gloucester, Captain Doug McLean, built by Tarr and James at Essex in 1893. Photographer Albert Cook Church of New Bedford is along, around 1906. The men raise the seineboat, which is thirty-six feet or longer, off the deck with tackles from the mastheads and have to work it out between the shrouds, which are less than thirty feet apart, before lowering away with a nice sense of timing to hold it from whacking against the side when the vessel rolls. (Albert Cook Church, The Whaling Museum)

2. The seineboat has been let back abaft the main rigging on the port side, where the seine roller is customarily secured to the rail, and the twine is being fed over. The fleet hovers nearby. There must be mackerel around. Sometimes, while they were cruising for mackerel, they towed the loaded seineboat alongside but at a distance from an outrigger. (Albert Cook Church, The Whaling Museum)

3. Not so merry are these mackerelers hunched around the potbellied stove in this rare vignette of the main cabin of a mackerel schooner, the *John D. Long,* built by Willard A. Burnham at Essex in 1880. Democracy was the rule aboard Gloucestermen, as many as could fit bunking with the Old Man aft. Above the deck level to the left of the companionway is the compass compartment, giving the helmsman his course from the wheel and the skipper a check on it practically from his bunk. The coal scuttle sits on a trap door leading to the coal locker below. (Goode's *Fisheries*)

125

1

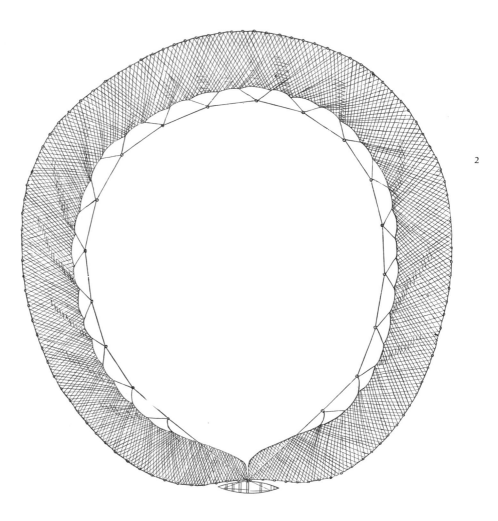

2

126

3

1 "Row like hell, boys!" Mackerel have been spotted, the men have leapt over the rail into *Pinta*'s seineboat, two more into the dory, and they're off. That looks like the school rippling the water over there beyond the bow fifty yards, where the skipper is pointing. Just ahead of the seine-master struggling with his sixteen-foot steering oar, the pump sticks up; a wet seine brings aboard a lot of water. (Albert Cook Church, The Whaling Museum)

2. The fully extended mackerel purse seine, drawn by Captain Collins, buoys around the greatest circumference, weighted purse line ready to be drawn through the snatch blocks into the seineboat lying at the narrow bunt end of the net. (Goode's *Fisheries*)

3. Having encircled the school and returned to the dory holding one end of the bunt, oars racked up out of the way, the merry mackerelers bend to the bridle with a will, and the urgent pursing begins. Their schooner hangs by in the sole care of the cook. Will the school hold in there, or dive and escape? (Goode's *Fisheries*)

1

2

1, 2. The seine has been pursed around a good school after all. *Pinta* has sailed alongside, and the cork line has been taken over the rail and stoppered. Gradually the net has been "dried up" until *Pinta*'s seineboat is almost alongside, held off with oars at bow and stern to leave room for the dipping. Now the long-handled scoop net is lowered by tackle into the flipping, flashing mass of mackerel, coming up with a barrel or two at a dip to add to a mighty, and deepening, deckload. (Albert Cook Church, The Whaling Museum)

3. With foresail down and out of the way to clear the decks amidships, *Pinta* lies to under main and jumbo. The "splitting keelers" and "gib keelers" have been set up on butts, and the gang has been splitting and "gibbing" all night. The splitter knifes each mackerel cleanly down the back, as many as sixty a minute, and tosses it to his gibber, who cleans out the guts with a sweep of his gloved fingers (the bones are sharp) and flings the fish into a "wash barrel" half-filled with sea water; when the barrel is full of fish, the water is poured off and clean sea water and salt are added — a barrel of salt to four of mackerel. On this voyage, the first lot was iced down below "in the round" without splitting, and the rest of it was salted in the butts on deck. (Albert Cook Church, The Whaling Museum)

1. Captain McLean puffs on his clay pipe and ponders the price such a full fare will fetch back home as *Pinta* fills away for Gloucester wing-and-wing (or "wung out"), foresail to port, mainsail to starboard. The last of the barrels is being headed; they will be opened upon arrival, and the mackerel resalted for market. (Albert Cook Church, The Whaling Museum)

2. Postscript to merry mackereling: no mere summer sailer, *Pinta* lies at the wharf of the Atlantic Halibut Company after a bitter trip dory-trawling for halibut. She had an unusually long and unusual life for a Gloucester schooner — sold down to Newfoundland on the eve of World War I and winding up as a floating yacht clubhouse in Chicago. (Martha Hale Harvey, Thomas Collection)

8. THE MERRY MACKERELERS

Then it's laugh, "Ha! ha!" and shout, "Hurrah!"
We are bound for the coast of Maine;
Our hold is well stored with salt and food,
In the boat we've a fine new seine.

The sun goes down as we round Eastern Point —
For Monhegan our course is laid;
The watch is set — the pipes are lit,
And a game of cards is played.

— From "The Merry, Merry Mackerel Catchers" by Jacob S. Lord.
In *The Fishermen's Own Book*, 1882.

There may have been some poetic license in measuring the merriment of the mackerel catchers, but there is no doubt that the summertime game of hide-and-seek with that streak of striped lightning, *Scomber scombrus*, was a very different kettle of fish from the all-season, all-weather battle to extract mighty *Hippoglossus hippoglossus*, *Gadus morrhua* and *Melanogrammus aeglefinus* (not to mention *Merluccius bilinearis*) from the murky depths.

If mackereling was not quite a yachting vacation, there were compensations for the hard-bitten Georgesman in taking to the summer seas with the companionable fleet under all sail and a skyful of stars, as there were supposed to be, anyway, for college boys signing on to be made men of. In 1870, when my namesake grandfather joined a crew of seventeen on board a large Gloucester mackerel schooner for a summer vacation trip following his freshman year at Harvard, the day of the jiggers, though waning, was still in pretty full swing. J. Everett Garland, eighteen, of Gloucester, packed along his journal:

Left port between 10 and 11 Wednesday. Out of sight of land before sundown. Feel a little qualmish but not much. Saw two whales about a mile from vessel. Saw a school of blue fish. Wind shifted from SW to SE, not blowing very strong. Running about 6 knots an hour. Like on the water much.

Thursday. Dont feel quite as well as I did yesterday. Have not yet vomited though constantly in fear of it. Dont eat much. Dont like looks of "Salt Horse," old potatoes etc. I sit generally all day or part on the wheel box. The Captain talked all feeling of sickness away last night & had a pleasant night's rest. Captain says we shall see "Georges" tonight. I didnt take any dinner today.

Friday. "Mackerel, mackerel," greeted my ears at an unusually early hour (about 4). I hastily dressed & found all busily fishing on deck. My barrel was placed behind me, to throw my fish into, "strike barrel" they call it. I was soon busy at work and caught less than ¼ bbl, about ¼ as much as some. My position is last aft except boy over the davit. I like fishing well enough but hate dressing. Eben Bray and I dress together. He splits, I "gib." He ploughs and then we salt down. One wash barrel makes generally about ¾ of a salt barrel after they have withered.

Caught more mackerel this afternoon & I got quite tired before through & repented my ever leaving shore. I think I was rather rash.

Saturday. Again my early slumbers disturbed by that to me this day almost hateful cry "mackerel, mackerel." Hastily dressing & in no pleasant mood I obey the unwelcome summons & soon am busy, but still with the constant thought in my mind "What a fool I was to leave shore."

Lines get tangled. Fish enough to fill a barrel, it seems, drop from my line when nearly in the barrel & I grow almost angry seeing so many "midships" catching so large a quantity. I cant take things here easy enough & I grow discontented. We got through last night at 11 o'clock & it seemed as though I hadnt been sleeping but half an hour. The wind is quite fresh E. I believe 'tis foggy & I hope we wont catch any fish tonight.

No fish have been caught & I am SO glad. There is a very heavy swell as though it had been blowing a gale, 10 to 15 feet high.

Sunday. Oh blessed thought. Nothing to do today. Didnt get up til after 7, I believe. Beans for breakfast. Beans dont set well on my stomach. Captain had services in the forecastle this morning. The cook & Captain sing, though Capt's voice is rather cracked.

The journal ends here, but Grandfather made a college paper of it from which his further adventures can be picked up (polished up) at anchor on Georges Bank in twelve fathoms:

As we had a cod line with us, I assayed my luck, and with 16 pounds as a sinker paid out 120 fathoms or over 700 feet of line. Twice did I pull up this entire length assured of a fish, and twice was I disappointed, the weight of the line and the lead causing my blunders.

The third time, long before I had wound in half my line, my arms were tired, but with assistance I kept up courage, and after a while with line and gaff we secured our fish, a noble halibut full four feet long. And a jolly time we had with it!

We were now bound for Prince Edward Island, Bay St. Lawrence and then home. Without accident we traversed the whole distance, fared sumptuously on the provisions of PEI, hunted to a small extent in Labrador and fishing when we desired. Always had a fresh supply on hand, especially of mackerel.

When we had seen all that was wonderful, had gazed upon and feared the icebergs, we left these pleasant scenes and, passing through the Straits of Canso, in four days were home, wafted by a breeze that at every puff lay our gallant craft well on her side and bellied her sails to the full.

With sorrow I left her and parted from my companions with whom for six weeks I had shared the pleasures and dangers — for there were dangers — of our trip. The extreme heat of the summer had passed, and I had returned just in time to begin the winter's work.

As Grandfather got his sea legs, the mackereling apparently ended merrier than it began. Old ocean was not for him, however, and back in Gloucester he would follow in his father's footsteps as a doctor — and not the cooking kind, either. Twelve years after this maritime experiment he completed his medical education abroad and returned home to assume his father's practice while the senior Doctor Garland served as mayor. In honor of the occasion the fishing firm of Cunningham and Thompson in 1882 had Moses Adams build the eighty-ton schooner *J. E. Garland*, which joined the *Joseph Garland* in the fleet.

The purse seine had displaced the mackerel jig so decisively by 1881 that only two Gloucester vessels bothered to go handlining in the once-popular Bay of St. Lawrence that year, and they returned with fewer than fifty barrels between them.

Summer breezes, shirt-sleeves weather, longer days, balmy evenings and cool nights, the camaraderie of large crews, sailing hither and yon in company with a spread-out flotilla of six or seven hundred schooners sometimes, friendly and not so friendly rivalries and the excitement of impromptu races add up to an impression of lighthearted fishing in those years of abundance when the silvery mackerel schooled from horizon to horizon, challenging their merry pursuers to dip them from the sea for the delectation of half the world.

Although many of the Gloucester seiners were refitted out of other fisheries for the season, plenty were custom-built for owners and masters, such as Captain Solomon Jacobs, "King of the Mackerel Killers," who were bold specialists in the fishery and always experimenting with new boats, new means of propulsion, new methods, and looking for new grounds.

These schooners had extra-wide decks for extra-big deckloads of fish and were designed for speed on the old caution: first to market gets the top dollar. Joseph Collins believed they spread more sail for their size than any other vessels in the world except the extreme schooner yachts of American and European millionaires. The technique of seining, the dressing of the

133

sometimes huge fares and the extra sail-handling called for big crews, usually fourteen men, taking it easier after a hard winter dory-trawling to the eastward or handlining on the Georges, and a few college boys or other young fellows on what they had been led to imagine would be an easy-money cruise.

After rendezvousing to the southward off the Chesapeake for the first run of the spring, the mackerelers followed the schools ever north and east along the coast in ravenous packs. Gloucestermen dominated completely, joined by schooners from ports large and small from Jersey to Maine. What a panorama this great fleet presented when, as if marshaled by an impulse kindred to the instinct that shifts a school of mackerel quixotically in this direction or that, they headed as one for the same harbor for the night! This occurred one unforgettable September afternoon away back in 1848. As birds of a feather, the fleet was joined by a flock of coasting schooners, and someone was there on the harbor shore to record the scene for the *Gloucester Telegraph*:

The two greatest sailing matches ever known in this country came off in this bay and harbor on Wednesday afternoon and Thursday morning. The prize on Wednesday afternoon was the best anchoring ground. Between 3 and 4 o'clock that afternoon the vessels began to make their appearance off the Point, coming in with a fair breeze from the south. From the time mentioned until long after dark, there was one continued string of schooners coming into the harbor, and at dark it was estimated there were 500 vessels inside of Eastern Point! At times there were from 100 to 150 vessels under sail between the Fort and the Point; and they would come into the harbor four and six abreast — even when it would be supposed that there was scarcely room for another vessel to anchor. It was certainly one of the most magnificent views of the kind we ever witnessed.

By eleven the next morning the last of this armada had upped anchor, made sail and rounded the Point for the eastward — but the wind came ahead Friday morning and three hundred were back in the harbor to await a favorable shift. At the final count, three schooners had managed to run ashore, and six thousand fishermen and sailors. The schooners were got off with little damage, likewise the men. The *Telegraph* breathed a sigh of relief after it was all over: they were a pretty good crowd after all — not overly drunk, surprisingly few brawls.

Making passage, the larger Gloucester mackerelers of eighty or a hundred years ago usually towed their seineboats unless on a long trip, when they might be hoisted aboard. The two dories were sometimes pressed into service on deck and filled with the surplus of fish if all the barrels had been topped off at the end of the trip, and harbor was almost in sight. Whether stowed on deck on a raised grating between the cabin house and the after fish hatch or in the seineboat while under tow, the bulky net had to be regularly salted down to keep it briny and moist as guard against rot and spontaneous combustion of the compacted twine, tar-impregnated and highly flammable when dry.

Once on the grounds, the merry mackerelers cruised about with one or two sharp-eyed spotters at the mastheads searching for the telltale signs of the schooling fish before the surface of the water betrayed their presence — clues such as whales, porpoises or gannets feeding on them or competing for lesser prey — or signs, simply, of other vessels preparing to set. The "fishy" members of the crew, who were said to be able to smell a school if it was anywhere around, were also eyed for evidence of olfactory agitation. Schools "cartwheeling" or milling around in tight circles while feeding were preferred as easier to encircle, besides being more preoccupied.

When the lookout hollered and skipper had satisfied himself that it was a good chance, he ordered his men into the seineboat. The ensuing excitement was described by an observer on a Gloucester mackereler around 1880:

As a pack of school boys jump from an apple tree when the indignant owner appears, so eleven men leap into the seineboat one over another, as if they had meant to jump overboard but by accident had reached the seineboat instead. The captain takes his place at the steering oar. Two men sit on the forward part of the seine and are at the cork line, ready to "throw out the twine" when the captain gives the word of command. The remaining seven row swiftly and silently until the fish disappear or the captain orders them to "stop rowing." All the while the captain is eagerly watching the fish, noticing which way they move and how fast.

Calculating the extent of the school and gambling on the mass complacency or uncertainty that might chance to hold it there long enough to be entrapped, the captain exhorts his men to row like the very devil around this rippling, seething spot on the surface of the sea, while the trio manning the seine feeds it overboard in the wake of the surging boat. Over goes the mass of twine, twenty fathoms deep at its deepest at the bunt, from sinker-weighted lead line up to the buoying cork line, a skirt two hundred fathoms round, twelve hundred feet, encircling the indecisive school.

Two more crew have been following along in one of the dories, and when skipper shouts and the end of the seine hits the water, they grab the start of the cork line and hold on while the seineboat pulls away for the encirclement of the fish.

Within a few minutes, if all goes right, the seineboat has completed the set and is back alongside the waiting dory with the other end. The cork line, lead line, bridle and the ends, which are the finish of the taper from the bunt through the wings and half its depth, are united. The dorymen jump into the seineboat. The two ends of the bridle, which is the line running free through the pursing rings secured at intervals to the lead line, are instantly

THE MERRY MACKERELERS

rove through the snatch blocks in the bow and stern of the seineboat, and the crucial pursing begins.

Every second counts now. Six on one end of the bridle, seven on the other, they haul in like madmen, drawing the bottom of the seine into an ever-tightening circle under the school, closing the trap. "A man who won't pull every pound he can and an ounce more," goes the old saying of the seiners, "isn't fit to be a fisherman."

In ten minutes or so from the skipper's first shout to throw out the twine, the purse has been drawn. Now the shallow end of the seine is hove dripping aboard the seineboat — "drying up," they call it — herding the bewildered mackerel into the deep bunt end.

All by himself back aboard, the cook has been keeping the schooner laid to, watching it all intensely, and now brings her up alongside the pursed seine if the breeze is light enough. If not, three or four row the dory over, get aboard, and give him a hand. This is a touchy piece of seamanship, requiring judgment and finesse.

The cork line is taken up over the vessel's rail and made fast by stoppers, and the drying-up is resumed until the net, now much reduced in volume, is jammed close between schooner and seineboat, aquiver with claustrophobic mackerel. If the prey dive and press too hard on the bottom of the net, threatening to burst through, cook may duck below for a hod of ashes from his stove, which he dumps overboard; the whitish appearance of the water is sure, 'tis said, to frighten them back to the surface.

And now the payoff. The big dip net is rigged to the main and forestaysail halyards, and three or four of the gang jump to the lines. The dip is lowered into the swarming school, skipper managing the long handle and giving the orders. They haul away and up comes half a barrel of the squirming objects of it all. Over the rail with them, deftly dump them in silvery disarray on the deck, and back over with the dip for the next.

Every once in a while the skipper's eye, or his luck, proved bigger than his seine. When his deck was alive from rail to rail with all the mackerel he could manage — or even dress expeditiously, for they spoiled fast in warm weather — and more to come, he might raise a flag to his masthead as invitation to his nearest less fortunate rival to sail over and join in the bounty, for shares, or for nothing if he and his crew were feeling that openhanded.

Such largesse was harder to come by after 1880, with the invention of the mackerel pocket, or spiller, an immense net bag lowered over the side and kept in position in the water by outriggers. Over into this could be spilled two hundred or more barrels of fish from the seine, keeping them alive until there was room on deck to dress them and freeing the net for another set.

As a rule, in fact, the net results of a day's labors in the seineboat ranged from fairly good to indifferent to bad to even worse. A week or so after dropping Eastern Point astern in the *William S. Baker* back in the 1870s, as already related, the Norwegian fisheries expert Fred Wallen had his first experience of Yankee mackereling off the coast of Maine, illustrating that the fisherman's best-laid schemes, if based on a worn-out seine, gang aft a-gley.

A large school was spotted from the *Baker*. It took thirty minutes to row out. They set around it and pursed in, they figured delightedly, three hundred barrels of mackerel. The schooner was brought alongside and had dipped out fifty when the rest of the school, rushing around wildly, burst the twine in several places and escaped.

They dressed the catch, repaired the seine, and next day, bright and early at six, set and caught nothing, set again at eight, and the whole school sank and made off, tried again at eleven — and though "as far as we could see on all sides they were playing on the surface of the water," caught eight fish. Thrice more that afternoon the Gloucestermen set for a total of about twelve barrels.

Discouraged but not daunted, Captain Albion K. Pierce was after a school next morning at the crack of dawn, and it escaped. An hour later he set once more around an enormous school of large, fat ones — close to five hundred barrels, they were sure. The *Baker* sailed up, the edge of the bunt was dragged up over the rail and the dipping was about to commence:

But the fish were very uneasy in the seine; sunk to the bottom with such force that the boat was on the point of capsizing, although we placed eight men on the other gunwale to counterbalance the mackerel. At one time all went smoothly enough to haul in on the seine and make the purse smaller and smaller to prevent the frantic rushing of the mackerel. But suddenly they sank again to the bottom, careened the boat over so that we took in a quantity of water.

We were scarcely ready to place ourselves on the other gunwale when we felt that the boat suddenly righted itself and lay still. The most knew what had happened; it was that the mackerel succeeded in breaking the old seine. Through a large hole, which became larger and larger, about the whole school escaped; and although we in all haste hauled in on the fragments and tried to form a new purse, we succeeded in saving not more than five in the whole 500 barrels.

The disgusted Captain Pierce took aboard his useless seine, which he had to admit was now past mending, raised sail and in a few hours was in Boothbay Harbor, where he put his Norwegian guest ashore to return to Gloucester by steamer and rail, impressed by the possibilities of the new American twist on the fishing, and in the caution implicit in the ditty:

Our hold is well stored with salt and food.
In the boat we've a fine new seine.

9. HOME IS THE SAILOR

One of the most exciting scenes imaginable is that of a fleet of hundreds making the port [Gloucester] in a storm. In a northeast gale they must beat in. All day long, by two and threes, they come. It is luff, bear away, or tack ship to avoid a smash. Crack, snap, goes a jib-boom off. Crack, snap, there is one main-boom the less. Hoarse voices of the skippers howl in entreaty or command above the howling gale, and the shore is lined with listening lookers-on.

— From *Century Magazine*. In *The Fishermen's Own Book,* 1882.

A fishing trip might last three days or six months, but it was not over until you were back snug in Gloucester, tied up to your wharf or safely at anchor, whether after two weeks of battling headwinds the whole way from the Grand Bank or a few hours' run around from Ipswich Bay. For all its size and openness, the harbor could be right tricky to make.

Barring a sudden squall, or rolling fogbank or disappearance of the breeze, the returning Gloucesterman was more or less home in a breeze once someone spotted the welcoming hump of Rockport's Pigeon Hill on the horizon. After dark the unmistakable twin flashes of Cape Ann Lights on Thacher's Island off Rockport assured the skipper that he was pretty near there. Having fetched them, however, he must keep offshore long enough to bring open Eastern Point Light, which he must drop behind on his starboard quarter before hauling his sheets for Gloucester Harbor. Once around Eastern Point, the returning schooner took care to steer well clear of the spar buoy marking the western end of the long and lurking shoal of Dog Bar that reached almost halfway across the harbor entrance before the granite breakwater on top of it was completed in 1905.

Inside the outer harbor, transient coasting schooners and such usually anchored on the Pancake Ground, a stretch of good flat holding bottom under the western lee of Eastern Point. The fishermen generally sailed on in past Ten Pound Island to the inner harbor and their home wharves or anchored in the stream and called for a tow the last few hundred yards after the skipper had found a dealer to buy his fish.

One of the more virtuoso performances in this line was credited to Captain George Melville (Mel) McClain, fisherman and schooner designer extraordinary, by the author Wesley G. Pierce. McClain's most famous design was the little *Lottie S. Haskins*, prototype of a fleet of sisters, built for him by Tarr and James in Essex in 1890. She was regarded as one of the most perfectly balanced schooners ever to sail in or out of Gloucester, on all points of the wind except in a dead calm.

Amazed by the *Haskins* himself, Mel was bound in to Gloucester with a trip of mackerel one day, the wind dead against him, and announced to the gang, as Pierce tells it:

"Boys, I'm going to try this vessel today an' see just what she will do!" So the skipper gave his orders and his crew carried them out as follows:

"Clew up th' tops'ls! Take in th' balloon-jib, an' furl 'er up! Let th' flying-jib run down! Take in th' mains'l, an' furl 'er up, boys! Let your jib run down! Take in th' fores'l!"

After these orders had been given and carried out, the *Haskins* was luffed up close around the Point, and all the *sail* she then had *set* was her fisherman's *stays'l*. Under this one small sail alone, Mel McClain beat the *Lottie S. Haskins* up into Gloucester Harbor and put her alongside the wharf, a most remarkable performance, and the *only vessel* ever able to do it, so far as I know.

Shooting right up to the wharf and coasting to a stop on a dime to the delight of the crew and the spectators was a matter of professional pride with the old-time skippers. Captain Collins had done his share of showing off in this regard and advised on the fine points. When the wind is blowing from the wharf, said he, keep under sail and hold your headway as you approach from the leeward.

The head sails are then hauled down and she is luffed to the wind, after which the mainsail is lowered. It is customary at such times for the skipper to take a station where he can command the scene. An experienced man is placed at the wheel, who steers the vessel in conformity to the orders of the captain. Other men stand by with ropes to throw out as the vessel approaches the wharf, these being fastened by persons on the wharf in readiness to receive them. The headway of the vessel is thus checked and she drops into her berth.

To shoot into a wharf with a free wind all sails are hauled down while the vessel is yet some distance from it and she is allowed to run in with bare poles. This, however, can only be accomplished with safety when there is a comparatively moderate wind, or when perhaps the tide is partially ebbed, so that the vessel may bring up on the bottom. It is by no means an unusual occurrence for a vessel to shoot alongside of a wharf with her mainsail, and sometimes her foresail, up when the wind is blowing from it.

And then there was the day in the 1930s when the last of the great schooners, the *Gertrude L. Thebaud*, was approaching her berth under sail. It must have been a high-course tide, for according to the version I heard there was some little miscalculation at the wheel, or possibly a slight shift in the breeze. She failed to come around quite quickly enough and ran her bowsprit through the window in the office on the end of the wharf in a crash of glass, missing the nose of the startled secretary by a few inches; no further harm done. So goes the story, anyway.

All of this fancy work at the wheel and the sheets depended, naturally, on some wind, which of course meant that the breeze that at one moment was winging the well-laden Gloucesterman home to port might at the next tire of the game and abandon the plaything, as gently as if it were a waif, on the doorstep of the harbor — sails limp, gaffs swinging overhead in the roll of the swell — and steal away. In such a fix, after much hemming and hawing, staring aloft, examining the glassy water off to the eastward for signs of new air, stroking of beards and conferring around the wheelbox, the skipper with a fresh trip of fish looking for a respectable price, and men anxious to get back ashore, would decide the fee was worth it and order the towboat signal run up in the rigging.

Like the owners who built glassed-in "crow's nests" on top of their buildings where spotters could watch for their returning vessels, the tow-boat captains kept a lookout above the steamship wharf where they tied up. When a fisherman becalmed off the end of the Point with his signal up, or a salt ship or a coaster was spied through the glass, out would churn the old *Joe Call*, the *Emma Bradford*, or *S. E. Wetherell*, *Nellie*, *Startle*, or *Mariner*, or later one of Captain Charles T. Heberle's succession of them, *Charlie*, *Priscilla* or his last and most prized, *Eveleth*.

When the late James E. Brennan of Gloucester was a boy in the years preceding the First World War, his Uncle Israel Crosby was engineer on the *Eveleth*, and Andy Jacobs was skipper.

Summers when school was out I'd take my uncle's lunch down to the boat to him, and sometimes he'd say, "Well, you can git a ride to Boston today." Going up, it would be a schooner with fish, lined up for a higher price in Boston than Gloucester. Or maybe we'd pick up a vessel had taken out at Boston and wanted to get home quick, because we could do twelve knots and they couldn't hold to that the whole way under sail. I think the *Eveleth* only got about a hundred dollars for the tow, so it was worth it if there was enough price difference on the fish.

To bring 'em home, we'd pick 'em up at T Wharf where they took out. Most generally have to wait for some of the crew to come down from uptown. We'd pull away from the wharf amidships of the vessel, with lines fore and aft to her, and when we got around by Deer Island, say Nixes Mate, we'd shift over to the long tow, with the hawser dippin' in the water astern. Captain Jacobs would holler through his megaphone, "Heist yer fores'l!" to ease the strain of the tow, and they'd heist their fores'l.

There was some fun and excitement one time I remember, comin' down, they'd probably had a few drinks uptown, and after they heisted their fores'l they decided to heist their mains'l too, and they did. Well, pretty soon the schooner was sailin' along, with the hawser splashin' through the water between us, right abreast of our pilot house, and Jacobs was hollerin' through his megaphone, and everybody excited, "Take in yer mains'l! Take in yer mains'l!"

So rarely were any means but steam or patience resorted to by becalmed skippers before the auxiliary engine changed it all that Douglas Parker could recall vividly after sixty years the exceptional day a haddocker, whose master was possibly too nigh to pay the towing fee, was hauled all the way in from the breakwater by her dories.

Before the days of mechanical refrigeration and quick-freezing, as many as sixteen million pounds of fresh fish, mostly halibut, were landed annually and shipped out of Gloucester in ice. What counted were the fastest passage back from the grounds and no hanging around in the harbor, fast taking-out and processing, and fast work teamstering the fish to the depot for the next train or to the steamship wharf for the *City of Gloucester*, destination Boston and points south and west.

At the head of the fleet were the catchers and purveyors of King Halibut, whose regime was to be all too brief. Unless owned by the Atlantic Halibut Company, the returned halibuter anchored in the stream and the skipper rowed ashore, called around for the best price he could dicker, rowed back and sailed or was towed in to his buyer's wharf.

No sooner alongside than the hatches were opened, the halyards were swung over, and the big ones were being hoisted tail first out of the ice bins by the lumpers and up to the wharf, where the shoresmen decapitated, weighed and culled them white or gray according to their undersides, gray getting the lesser price by far although there wasn't a particle of difference in the flesh.

This particular practice of cheating the fishermen originated with the Gloucester Halibut Company, organized by the dealers in 1848 to fix prices on an incredible run of the fish on Georges Bank. The firm invented the color test to subvert its contracts with the fishermen. One day that spring twenty Georgesmen were tied up at the company's wharf or waiting to get in with a million pounds of fresh halibut. Result: a glutted market, no buyers, no price, and they had to dump most of it outside Eastern Point. The company succumbed to its own greed after only four months, but the color rip-off lived on until the overfished species very nearly died off.

The Gloucester dealers had another trick. They unilaterally designated

141

fourteen percent of the halibut's weight for the head, which they deducted from the price paid for every fish, although everyone knew the head comprised a smaller proportion, particularly as the fish increased in size. The heads thus stolen were sold by the dealers for fertilizer and industrial oil. The fish were boxed, iced and shipped. Some fresh and some flitched (split and salted) halibut were diverted to the smokehouse and sold in various grades.

With the halibuters it was fast work. The record for unloading and processing a trip was set at Atlantic Halibut in 1879 — 103,000 pounds from the schooner *William Thompson* in eight hours. The biggest fare, 137,510 pounds, was landed by the *Centennial* from a four-week trip in 1877. That was the peak, and the species, slow-growing and clannish in its habits, could not hold its own against the concentrated overfishing.

With minor exceptions the "lay" on the halibuters was typical of the traditional profit-sharing system of the Gloucestermen, save for the haddockers. From the gross stock, which was the whole amount received for the fare of fish, the owners deducted the cost of ice, bait, towage and the dorymen's woolen nippers, but paid for food and fishing gear. The remaining net was split fifty-fifty between the vessel (the owners) and the crew, including captain and cook, after deducting from the crew's share charges for filling the freshwater casks, splitting stovewood, replenishing the medicine chest, tarring, rigging, painting spars, and one-half of one percent for the Gloucester Fishermen's and Seamen's Widows and Orphans Aid Society fund.

(Hence the honored motto of the dorymates: "Share and share alike." It was according to this code that Atlantic Halibut, taking into account his failure to "earn" his full share due to circumstances beyond his control, paid the crippled and broke Howard Blackburn on his return to Gloucester his due from the trip of the *Grace L. Fears*, $86.)

As a rule the captain of a fresh halibuter in addition received four percent of the net stock. The cook got extra pay on top of half of anything he caught over the rail on a handline or with his "bull tow," a short trawl with fifteen or twenty hooks trailed off astern while at anchor.

Half shares was the usual division of the pie on the dory trawlers and seiners. The haddockers, those hard-driven, all-weather commuters between the banks of Georges or La Have and Gloucester or Boston, worked on quarter shares by which the vessel drew a quarter of the net stock after deduction for bait, ice, wharfage and towage, including the skipper's percentage, and the crew three quarters; but the boys supplied their own dories and gear and paid for their grub. Aboard the Georgesmen the crew's share was prorated between high line and low line for the trip, according to the tally of codfish tongues each man turned in back at the wharf.

The average Gloucester fisherman in 1879 made $175, although the Goode study estimated that if he worked like the devil for twelve months, including winter, he stood to earn as much as $300 to $500, the skipper usually double that.

By the share system, the owners risked their vessels and the capital tied up in the trip; the men risked their lives and their livelihoods. The profits of a good trip were shared by all. The loss incurred in a broker, a profitless trip, was absorbed by the owners, and sometimes by the builder, who might still be waiting for his money; the men got a bunk and, except on the haddockers, their grub out of it, and plenty of fresh air, and charged the family's food, clothing, medicine and frequently rent to the owner's store or account, hoping against hope to get out of debt the next trip — if they got out of it alive.

"There is little evidence, however, that the capitalists are to blame for this," rationalized the Goode Report, "since they are quite as dependent upon the vicissitudes of the fisheries as the men to whom they supply the means of carrying on the actual work."

Similarly, Gloucester boardinghouse keepers were permitted legally to "trustee" their unmarried fisherman tenants, that is, to attach their shares when they were fresh off the boat, lest they be tempted to run out on their bills.

With the accelerating extermination of the Atlantic halibut as a commercially significant species in the closing years of the last century, and the cyclical withdrawal of the seemingly numberless mackerel schools (in some degree, surely, in self-defense), the sturdy old codfish, reliance of Gloucester from the beginning, once again assumed its former position.

Not to say that fresh mackerel did not continue in demand, mainly in the Boston market, iced in the round and direct from the holds of the speedy Gloucester seiners, but it is an oily fish and spoils rapidly. Salt mackerel, split, gibbed and graded, was only lightly pickled aboard and was resalted in Gloucester and shipped off in barrels, boxes and tins. However, as the supply declined, the taste for salt mackerel, and the demand, followed. Haddock remained the favorite fresh fish of the table, with hake far behind.

Occasionally a small schooner or sloop fitted out from Gloucester for the swordfishery, but most of these sleek giants with the lethal beaks were brought back in barrels, pickled, as an incidental dividend by mackerelers fitted with pulpits on their bowsprits from which the "striker" in the crew preached to the prey with his harpoon.

Because it was a relatively cheap protein that could be shipped anywhere in compact form and for all practical purposes in an indefinite state of preservation, salt codfish reigned as the popular choice and lifted Gloucester to world supremacy as the century turned.

Mass production did it, by way of the trawl line at one end and some classically simple Yankee inventiveness at the other. The inventor was George Smith, who around 1870 figured out that it was more attractive to skin, bone and tidily box the salt codfish for the market than to ship them off as great ugly carcasses fraught with cartilaginous needles and encased in something a good deal tougher than shoe leather. Then some other Edison of the waterfront thought up the fishcake, consisting of codfish and potatoes all ground up in a ball, ready to be spooned out of the can, fried and doused with ketchup. At first, naturally, all the other Gloucester dealers resisted, but pretty soon the public would have nothing but boneless cod and codfish balls, and that was that.

Thus when the hundreds of bankers and Georgesmen eased in and tied up at the scores of Gloucester salt-fish wharves, out came the split fish, already pretty well kenched down in the hold, the only difference being that the Georgies, on shorter trips, used less salt than the bankers. The fish were weighed and then scrubbed with brushes in a tank or an old dory sitting on the wharf, half full of water. Then to the salting building on carts and into the pickling butts for curing, and after the proper time again piled in kenches to press out the brine.

The final stage of his curing found Mr. Codfish back in the fresh air being laid out with hundreds of thousands of his brothers and sisters on the flakes of Gloucester, those elevated platforms of slats that were erected on every spare square foot of wharf, land and even rooftop flat enough to walk on along the waterfront. William S. Webber, Jr., knew the business intimately and reminisced how the fish "were spread on the flakes daily and were removed toward nightfall or on threat of rain. They were protected from too much sun by long rolls of canvas duck which could be spread speedily in the heat of the midday. The master of the flake yard could sense the weather; some days he knew would be good drying days, while others were unsettled in the early mornings and spreading would be delayed until conditions were right. Tending the flakes gave many hundreds employment and provided work for schoolboys during the summer vacations."

After drying, the fish went to the skinning loft, where the skins were removed. From there, as Webber remembered, they moved "to the cutters, or trimmers, who removed the larger bones and neatly trimmed the edges; then to the bone pullers, a highly skilled group of women who deftly pulled out the smaller bones with tweezers; finally to the pressers and packers, and the white salt cod was ready for shipment. Much of this was piecework, and the fastest and most skilled took home the highest pay checks." Gorton-Pew over a period of years bought up several of the smaller fish firms and came to dominate the fisheries with the biggest fleet of schooners and the greatest acreage of flake yards.

144

Forty years before young Bill Webber's waterfront days, in 1879, Gloucester was already packing off 14 million pounds of its widely advertised "boneless fish."

As for the famous fishcakes and their ingredients, he recalled that the Aroostook County potatoes brought down from Maine on the railroad by the carload were "in winter attended by young men who kept the car stoves burning to prevent the spuds from freezing. Some looked forward to this trip as an adventure, but the isolation of a closed freight car with no scenery to be seen lost much of its glamour after a few trips."

Unlike the pig, whose squeal, at least, fled the stockyard with his soul to porcine heaven, the silent fish was stripped of his all by the efficient Gloucester processors. Long before reaching port in the ignominious middle of a dripping kench, the codfish had been separated from its insides, which were tossed back whence it came, and its liver, which was consigned to one of the gigantic liver butts lashed to the front of the cabin house on the bankers.

As the oil "made out" to the surface of the bilious mass in the butt, it was dipped out into water barrels that were stowed below on the longer voyages. Back from shorter trips, the schooners were visited by the "liver men," with their barrels in their dories, who oared from vessel to vessel and bought the livers on the spot. The purified cod liver oil was sold to drug firms as a medicinal "lung strengthener," the heavier residue as industrial tanner's oil.

Among the noisome refiners of this humble by-product was Joe Norwood, whose bubbling vats down at the end of Norwood Court on the East Gloucester waterfront earned it the sobriquet of "Blubber Alley," which prompts a story from George H. Procter's *Fishermen's Own Book:*

"It may smell a little fishy, but you soon get used to it," said an old man who was trying out blubber on one of our wharves to a young dandy-looking chap, who thought the effluvia was "perfwectly horwid." "And then," continued the old man, "it brings in the crispy greenbacks, you know, and your father was one of the best blubber b'ilers I ever knew." The young man fidgeted a little with his kid gloves and cane, and then quickly passed up off the wharf. He didn't care about hearing the old "blubber and ile" man give him any further reminiscences of his family. It's the case with a good many nowadays. They like to spend the old man's money, but don't care to remember that the old gent ever went fishing or followed any of the honest occupations connected therewith.

And then there was fish roe, much of which found its way to France. Gurry was turned into fertilizer. The sounds, the lunglike air bladders of the cod and hake, were reduced to pure isinglass, or gelatin, in a local plant.

Finally the skins, bones and whatever else was left behind by the boneless fish plants were conveyed — dripping, odoriferous and offensive to maiden ladies who slammed their windows shut when they heard the carts coming — through the streets of the city and over the Cut Bridge to the large and mysterious establishment of the Russia Cement Company in West Gloucester for positively alchemic conversion into its famous Le Page's fish glue.

The emanations from the glue factory's tall smokestack announced to the nostrils of Gloucester more surely than any weather vane which way the wind was blowing that day, and that all was as right as it ought to be with the world's greatest fishing port.

Safe home from Georges Bank, *Canopus* sails in by the copper paint factory and Rocky Neck in the early 1900s. The dorymen are "stream buyers" after such odds and ends as sounds and livers. The familiar, stubby steam ferry *Little Giant* crosses astern on her well-plied route between the main waterfront, Rocky Neck and East Gloucester. *Canopus* was built in Gloucester in 1885. (Ernest L. Blatchford, Thomas Collection)

Gloucester was not all schooners. The fishing sloop *On Time* makes time inside Eastern Point past the Hawthorne Inn over the end of her long bowsprit, home from dory-trawling. There were thirty-six such "Gloucester sloop boats" in the fleet in 1909, besides 196 schooners. Most fished the near grounds, though *On Time*'s venturesome owner in her latter days, Captain Peter Johnson, took her swordfishing offshore as far as Georges Bank. Some had clipper bows, some were plumb stemmers such as *On Time*, thirty-eight feet, built down East at Boothbay, Maine, in 1894. Thirty or so years later Captain Johnson cut her in half and added about twenty feet to her middle. A later owner made a schooner of her, and a still later one wrecked her off Scituate. (Ernest L. Blatchford, Thomas Collection)

148

Back from winter trawling, the *Clara G. Silva* prepares to drop a dory off, most likely for the skipper to row ashore in search of the best price for his trip. They had a good breeze on the port tack, judging by the line of ice just below the starboard scuppers. Built by A.D. Story in 1906, the *Silva* lost ten men in a squall on Jeffrey's Bank the next year. There was a noticeable increase in the number of schooners with Portuguese names joining the fleet in the early 1900s, reflecting the growing prosperity of the Portuguese fishing families in Gloucester and the high regard in which the fishermen, most of them from the Azores, were held. (Chester N. Walen, Thomas Collection)

149

1. Dressed in their best, three of the crew pose up in the bow of the *Gertie E. Foster* at Gloucester in 1882. The mammoth cable is of a size to hold on to the anchor catted outside the rail. Aft of the foremast is the forecastle companionway, and to the starboard of that, the stovepipe from the galley, minus the elbow with opening directed aft to keep a downpour or boarding sea from dousing the cook's fire. Two men lean against the windlass; the third sits on the heavy, old-time, wooden jumbo sheet traveler later replaced by a shorter "horse" of iron bar when the jumbo club gave way to the full-length jumbo boom that was better adapted to self-tending and required less traveler span. The year after she was built by Joseph Story at Essex in 1874, the *Gertie E.* in ten trips grossed 666,168 pounds of halibut. George F. Wilson was lost from a dory from her on September 29, 1875. On November 6, 1877 while on the banks, Captain Joseph Campbell was killed when he fell to the deck from aloft. Not many years after this photograph was taken, the *Gertie E. Foster* was lost off Liverpool, Nova Scotia, with five lives. (U.S. Fish and Fisheries Commission, courtesy of Al Barnes and The Mariners' Museum)

2. The men of the *Willie M. Stevens* prepare to unload halibut at Gloucester, 1882. The schooner was the high-line fresh halibuter in 1880 when she was three years old, stocking $22,107, the crew's share averaging $706. Her skipper told Captain Collins that the halibut off the northwest coast of Newfoundland were so persnickety about bait that they would hardly touch any herring except from the Bay of Islands and Boone Bay. The *Stevens* was one of a fleet of six owned by George Dennis of East Gloucester. John White was washed overboard from the *Stevens* in January 1881. On December 5, 1897 the *Willie M. Stevens* was wrecked near Port la Tour, Nova Scotia, while seeking bait on a haddocking trip. No lives were lost. (U.S. Fish and Fisheries Commission, courtesy of Al Barnes and The Mariners' Museum)

1. Four old hands remove the seine from a seineboat alongside a Gloucester wharf at high water. The roller prevents snagging. The wooden pump is simply a bored cylinder with a leather valve at the bottom. (Thomas Collection)

2. The dory suffers the penultimate indignity (next to geraniums on the front lawn) — filled with water instead of afloat on it. The men are washing the salt out of the split fish just unloaded and weighed off in the scales on Walen's wharf. Then the catch will be resalted and spread to cure on the flakes. Ballast stones are piled on the wharf behind. (Ernest L. Blatchford, Thomas Collection)

3. The splitting gang on the wharf of George H. Perkins and Sons disposes of a fresh shore-fishing trip from the *Evelyn M. Thompson*, April 19, 1912. Duly salted, the catch will end up on the flakes. The bowspritless *Evelyn M.*, whose bow is just visible at right, is a knockabout designed by Tom McManus to do away with the "widowmaker" by elongating the bow, and hence the foredeck, thereby keeping the headsails inboard. Bringing the bow out to where the bowsprit formerly ended, of course, added very considerably to the building cost, and after a while the overhangs were shortened. (Eben Parsons, Cape Ann Historical Association)

3

᪥ Neat as a church picnic, acres of flakes command the wharves and proselytize the roofs of the Reed and Gamage plant of the Gorton-Pew Fisheries in East Gloucester. The curing salt fish are covered against the heat of a summer day in 1912. When rain threatened, off came the cloths, and the fish were gathered up and stacked under covering boxes at the ends of the flakes in double-time. A salt barque from Sicily loafs in the stream, airing her sails. (Eben Parsons, Cape Ann Historical Association)

154

The mass production of salt fish, such as at the plant of Shute and Merchant, put Gloucester on the global map. Here their skinning loft gang prepares one of the firm's specialties, Georges codfish, for shipment. "Largest Boneless Fish Establishment in the United States," boasted the partners a hundred years ago, advertising salt fish and smoked halibut. "We send no circulars and employ no drummers, thereby avoiding an interference with our wholesale customers' trade. All goods warranted as represented." (Cape Ann Historical Association)

1   2

156

1. Out from the soggy secrecy of the fog slips the new knockabout schooner *Natalie Hammond*, one of three built by Leonard McKenzie at Essex just before World War I. The year is 1914. Almost nonexistent are photographs of the era of sail on thick days, probably on the general principle: "Who the heck would be crazy enough to try to take pictures in the fog?" (Eben Parsons, Cape Ann Historical Association)

2. A study in nonchalance, *Monitor* slides out by Rocky Neck around 1901. (Ernest L. Blatchford, Thomas Collection)

1. Three Gloucestermen of the 1890s drowse at their wharves under the rising backdrop of the port surmounted by the towers of City Hall and the Baptist Church. A water sloop shares the dock on the left; the mast of a partially hidden Gloucester sloop boat is visible at the wharf of the Ice and Bait Company. (Martha Hale Harvey, Thomas Collection).

2. An anonymous clipper spreads her wings to dry at Jordan's wharf. The water sloop *Wanderer* (1881) and the schooner *Legal Tender*, built way back in 1868, lie motionless on the glassy cove. (Martha Hale Harvey, Thomas Collection)

3. The sloop *Wenham Lake*, down almost to the gunwales with more or less fresh water, sails sluggishly toward Five Pound Island after replenishing perhaps the *Mary F. Chisholm* in the foreground at Chisholm's wharf, next to Walen's wharf where flakes await a fare, or maybe the *Mary E. Cooney* lying on the outside of the Gardner and Parsons wharf. Early 1900s. Drowned dory-trawling from the *Chisholm* in December of 1878 were William Cole and Lemuel Hagan, and in August of the next year, David Morrison. (Al Barnes Collection, The Mariners' Museum)

158

1   2

3

1

🕊 *1.* The crew of the *Porter S. Roberts* takes in the slack, in waterfront parlance, between trips at the Pettingell and Cunningham wharf up in Harbor Cove early in the 1890s. Built by Arthur Story in 1882, the *Roberts* was abandoned at sea in a gale in 1894. The men took to the dories and were picked up. (Martha Hale Harvey, Thomas Collection)

🕊 *2.* Hauled up at Cunningham and Thompson's, the *Louise R. Sylva* dries her canvas and provides a dizzying view of the harbor on a fine day in 1913 for the fellow way up there on the main spreader. Down on deck someone is jiggling a halyard at his direction. A topmast, presumably the *Sylva*'s, lies on the wharf — whether about to be shipped or just sent down is anyone's guess. The *Sylva* was sold up from Provincetown about this time and is probably being refitted. Boston, Provincetown, Portland, New York, and to a lesser extent New Bedford, Chatham and a number of smaller ports were actively fishing in these days, and ownership of schooners shifted frequently between Gloucester and the competition. (Eben Parsons, Cape Ann Historical Association)

160

3

3. The *M.A. Baston* and *Ethel B. Jacobs* get painted on Parkhurst's railways at the foot of Duncan Street. Sol Jacobs commissioned Moses Adams to build the *Jacobs* in 1891 as one of his succession of successful mackerel seiners (note the roller on the port rail); she looks pretty new here. The older *Baston*, built at Gloucester in 1878, hove ashore at Brace Cove on the back of Eastern Point while returning from halibuting on the thick morning of September 27, 1890. Captain Thompson rowed ashore in a dory, walked a half a mile to the nearest telephone and summoned the tug *Emma Bradford*, which steamed around and hauled the *Baston* off, not much damaged. The cradles onto which the vessels were floated at high water were pulled up the ways by steam winches. Back in 1860 the charges in Gloucester were $10 for hauling and laying for one good working day, and $5 a day thereafter for vessels under a hundred tons. The railway still operates today. Jeremiah Haley and James Dunphy were lost in their dory from the *M. A. Baston* on February 3, 1882. (The Smithsonian Institution)

1

1. Topmasts recede in a high fog (or low overcast, as the natives call it) hanging over the Gloucester waterfront a hundred years ago. A mackerel schooner tries droopily to dry out on the other side of a trim sloop with long, overhanging boom; the neat sail cover and the clean line of cabin trunk and coaming mark her as a yacht. Two or three of the "wharf rats" playing in the dories in the dock will be oaring them across the banks in ten more years. (Martin Horgan Collection)

2. *Nellie* is the epitome of the compact, powerful steam tug of yore as she bustles about the inner harbor. A salt ship off to the left looks sufficiently lightened to be towed over to Parsons salt wharf at East Gloucester, visible behind *Nellie*'s lifeboat. *Nellie* is in smart shape and was photographed not long after launching at Story's in 1902. Gloucester's first towboat of record was the *B.B. Gangloff*, built in 1869 and owned by her master, Captain Nicholas Gangloff, who offered "Towing, Watering and Steaming of Vessels." The installation of auxiliary engines in the schooners rapidly put the harbor tugs just about out of business. (Ernest L. Blatchford, Thomas Collection)

2

10. GLOUCESTER

Was there something almost equine about the schooners, a waiting dignity, a patient restlessness, a potential energy, as if vessels of wood were animated even at the wharf? At sea a fluctuating equilibrium prevailed between schooner and wind and wave under all but chaotic conditions, while at home, at ease, the recently plunging craft commanded the scene in silence and reigned over the stillness and fixedness of it.

As with familiar, saddle-broken horses and their riders — one who feels for boats knows instinctively — there was an implicit oneness between schooner and man. Out there the fishermen were in the rider's seat, urging on, reining in, driving, coaxing their gallopers. Back home in the old spot at the old slip it was all a fresh memory, and there was the comfortable entente of Jack leaning idly against the rail, butt to cap. Gloucestermen and Gloucesterman have been through more together than needs or wants the telling.

Even the towboats went about their busyness with the easy self-assurance of the veteran groom who knows his place in the hierarchy of the stable, managing, moving, harnessing, leading and holding back, by cajolery and persuasion.

No less did the schooners preside over their territory in the presence of the towering salt ships — great, dumb, dwarfing, domesticated oxen of the ocean alongside these thoroughbreds they had sailed across the sea to serve. So too with the coasting schooners of two, three, four, five and even six masts, the brigs and brigantines, the barks and the barkentines — mighty fancy rigs in the merchant service, but no match for the Gloucestermen in *their* port, or on the wind, or clawing across the Georges in a double-reef gale.

Only the dories, as straightforward and straightsided as the men themselves when it came to riding upon the crest of a wave, lived side by side or piggyback with the schooners of Gloucester in complete compatibility. Had it not been inherited by one generation after another of both breeds of boat, here was a symbiosis that would have had to be invented. That schooner and dory were inseparable, to their sailors and rowers, was as taken for granted as the primeval arrangement between shark and pilot fish, as if neither could manage for long without the other.

The very size and shape and smell of the Gloucester waterfront spelled *schooners*, was home to them, real home, always home from 1713 or thereabouts, anyway, which is long enough for the claim to become possession. Well, the waterfront certainly was all built and added on to, pieced together and replaced, to accommodate the rise and fall of the schooners with tide and time, and so were they. Naturally the wharves and the buildings were of wood so as not to offend the sensibilities of vessels that had been shaped by saw and plane from the woods out back. More symbiosis here.

Osmosis too, for the waterfront was and remains a membrane between the complicated and highly charged cellular metabolism of the city and what was once assumed to be the infinitely nutritious sea, the vital exchange between them carried on and moderated by the ebbing and the flowing, and the coming and the going.

Many of the parts of the Gloucester waterfront and its backdrop have changed, but the form hasn't much. It stays familiar between the tides of men's affairs. One of those faces frozen in the tapestried downtown studio of William Elwell, "photographist," thawed a hundred years later would crack into a slow smile of recognition. The timeless texture of the scene retains this uncanny quality of unchange as the town recedes before the gaze and rises through the streets and alleys in back and then up more sharply along the intimate and crowded slopes behind.

The prominent hills, Governor's and Portagee, are studded still with landmarks made famous by their durability, and durable by the famous like the native painter, Fitz Hugh Lane, and Winslow Homer, who was moved by what he saw and then moved on. There are not so many church spires, which is a sign of the times, but the most classic of them, and the oldest, that of the Universalists, has been pointing in the right direction for 180 years and still points. The blue twins of the Church of Our Lady of Good Voyage, the Portuguese fishermen's own, are less prominent but more arresting when discovered. Dominating everything in and out of sight since the Civil War, City Hall is the same disjointed Trojan horse, with its queer hips and shoulders, that it always has been.

Homer painted Gloucester the way Kipling wrote about it, from the outside in — tragic, stoic, but always energetic and dynamic. Lane viewed his world from the inside out, a spirit striving to release itself from a crippled body. He was the Blackburn of the brush, sworn to overcompensate he knew not quite for what. The one's single-minded paintings are as much a statement about Gloucester by indirection as the other's single-handed voyages. Fitz Hugh Lane was disabled, probably by polio, in his childhood and developed a Stevensonian feel for what he could not readily touch. His schooners and other sailing vessels at rest in his harbor are as delicately and yet definitely limned on canvas as if their images had been shed on a glass plate negative brushed with an emulsion of the finest grain. They have that in common with the photographs of Martha Hale Harvey. With that same palpability Lane caught the light from his heaven, and every nook and cranny of his harbor and his waterfront below his stone studio.

Fitz Hugh Lane, master of Gloucester's gentler ironies, froze in warmth the scene as he saw it, and as it emerged from him, and as it had been seen without much change for a hundred, two hundred years before he arrived upon it. And he passed the image on as heritage to the first photographers as they arrived upon it, almost precisely at his death in 1865, to do with it what they could and would, but not to improve, ever, on the Lane's-eye view of Gloucester, Massachusetts — only to build upon it.

A writer is at an impossible disadvantage when challenged with summoning up a word image of a place so seductive to the eye. I tried it twenty years ago, groping in *Lone Voyager* for the feel of the Gloucester to which Howard Blackburn had returned from his ordeal at sea in the spring of 1883, a hundred years ago:

Back in the recesses of the harbor, behind Ten Pound Island and Rocky Neck and Five Pound Island, by the Fort and Duncan Point, along Smith Cove and Vincent Cove and Harbor Cove, the shore sagged with wharves and shipyards, marine railways, chandleries and sail lofts, riggers, rope walks, net and twine factories, smithies, coopers and boxmakers, icehouses, warehouses, gashouses, paint shops, machine shops, sheds, stables, smokehouses, flake yards, oilskin makers, glue factories, fish dealers, salt dealers, outfitters, teamsters, brokers, agents, saloons, grogshops, poolrooms, barber shops, lunchrooms and boardinghouses.

The coarse redolence of flaked fish baking by the acre in the sun and the tang of tarred rope and nets and the pungency of fresh paint and the stink of the flats at low water and the iodine smell of the seaweed all mingled with the fresh salt air in an ambrosia of the sea. Floating arcs of snow, the gulls soared and wheeled and screamed, scavengers immaculate.

The schooners wedged in the wharves, stall after stall, like patient horses. They nudged and creaked against the pilings. The wavelets patted their sides and traded dancing shimmers of reflection with the mirrors of their sterns. The rigging sighed, and a block squeaked; a halyard slapped along a mast, and the drying sails rippled in the breeze.

Suddenly boys chased and yelled from deck to deck, scrambled panting up the shrouds, dove into the dark water, swam laughing to a hanging rope — underfoot, asking questions, watching, feeling the sea.

Men shouted and called, laughed, cursed, whistled. Iron rims rattled over cobblestones. Hammers argued with echoes of staccato. Steam hissed up into a fluff of cotton. A mallet clumped against a trunnel. A barrel clattered over a drum roll of loose boards. A cart thumped, a hatch slammed, chain clanked off a winch. And over it all the crying chorus of the gulls.

# 11. BETWEEN HOPE AND FEAR

"I tell yer what 'tis, this is a tough one. If this haint a regular old-fashioned screamer I never saw one."

> — About 9:00 p.m., February 10, 1879, aboard the Gloucester halibut schooner *Marion* on the Grand Bank of Newfoundland.

Gloucester was muffled up to its ears in it, winter after winter in those days, the drifts eight feet deep where the gale found a way to funnel down an alley. Sleighs swished and jingled over the hard pack, horses padding and puffing, the people stamping along the snow-steeped streets with crimson cheeks, bundled, noses dripping, breaths steaming. Down on the wharves the barrels, boxes, tubs, dories, unassorted gear and miscellaneous junk lay all anonymous under the blanket.

The schooners, some of them sheathed and sparkling in frozen sea spray half to their forepeaks, lay sealed solid and stolid in their berths. The salt ice shifted and hove and crackled and groaned with the muted tide out as far as the dazzled eye could squint beyond Five Pound Island and Rocky Neck and Ten Pound Island and beyond that, beyond Black Bess Rocks and beyond the very end of Eastern Point to the Reef of Norman's Woe. And the men in their greatcoats and thick hats and boots tramped out on their frozen harbor to their ice-locked schooners that needed no anchors for a while, slapping their mittened hands.

Up back in Gloucester the huddled houses with curls of smoke fighting the cold to get out of the chimneys, and the saloons with Jack Frosted windows, and the frigid waterfront, and the lifeless harbor itself were immobilized in the Arctic grip of an old-fashioned winter. Out there on the string of banks from Georges to the Grand, dodging the strays from the fringe of the ice floe, shouting imprecations in the teeth of the tempest, the Gloucestermen played cards by the heat of the cookstove, and games with the winter, chortled at it, shook their fists in the belly of it like hot Jonahs inside a cold whale. *That* was where the fish were, devil take the fish and us too.

166

Joseph William Collins was the only man alive, for sure, who could survive the full voltage of a lightning stroke while standing at the foot of his mainmast in a squall; the ball of fire knocked him sprawling and senseless, and they carried him below for dead.

Ah Collins, the great halibut killer, the fisherman of the ice pack, the adventurer, the oceanographer, the ichthyologist, naturalist, biologist, naval architect, reformer, pioneer, historian, museum curator, politician, polemicist and pamphleteer. Joe Collins, the grade school dropout from Maine, the Joe Conrad of the fisheries, so clear-eyed and clean-shaven above that wind-whipped mop of chin whiskers, who knew the worst out there as well as the rest and the best of them did. He wrote it, he did, the self-taught man, dog-tired down in his cabin, cold and wet, during snatches of rest from his watches on deck, all by lamplight in that precious log book of his.

Captain Collins has already given an account of the start of his halibuting trip to the Grand Bank in the schooner *Marion* at the beginning of 1879, when he was thirty-nine. It commenced well enough, as the reader will recall, with watches chosen by thumbing the hat after they had cleared Eastern Point, a sea making at bedtime, choppy and fretful, but not unusual for the season of the year. Let us pick them up again on their second day out, and sail along with them as it suits us, and shiver, and cease counting our blessings once and for all.

January 25, 1879: Soon after breakfast the hatches were taken off and the men took the trawls on deck and began rigging them up by bending the gangings, that had been unbent on the last passage home, into the beckets on the ground line. Each hook before being attached to the trawl undergoes a critical examination, and if dull must be touched up with a file, if crooked, straightened into proper shape, or, if the hook cannot be fixed so that it will serve all purposes, it is condemned and thrown aside . . . The trawls are marked in various ways with the number of the boat they belong to, and as they are passed on deck each dory's crew stand by to select or claim their own gear. When the marks happen to be indistinct on a good trawl, considerable discussion about the ownership frequently takes place . . . Some put in a claim, just for fun, to make the other claimants talk more earnestly; and considerable amusement is occasioned in this way, the non-contestants always urging on the others and laughing.

At last, all differences being satisfactorily settled, the men take up their stations on different parts of the deck, and the work of "fixing up" the trawls goes briskly on, many of the workers singing some ballad of the sea or telling their chums long stories of experiences which they met while last on shore.

January 26: It was bitterly cold all the morning and ice made rapidly on the deck and about the rigging. Nevertheless, we set the jib and riding sail soon after breakfast, and a half hour later saw a vessel at anchor ahead, which, as we approached nearer, we knew was the *Everett Steele*. There was no one to be seen on her deck, and as we passed close to her stern our men, most of whom had gathered aft on the quarter, joined in a general shout. This had the desired effect of frightening her crew, and four or five of the *Steele's* men rushed up, bareheaded and stockingfooted, to be greeted by the laughter and shouts of our fellows as we went dashing by. At 10 o'clock a.m. we passed a brig which was lying to under mainstaysail. She was badly iced up, and appeared to be laboring heavily, rolling her lee yard-arms nearly to the surface of the water.

To one standing upon the deck of our little schooner at this time, the scene, though grand and impressive, had a decidedly wintry and dreary look. The ice-covered hull and rigging, the dark masses of snow-laden clouds driven to leeward by the gale, which shrieked and whistled through the ropes and lashed into the wildest fury the foam-flecked waters, piling them into huge waves, was a sight that, once seen, could never be forgotten. But on we went, now plunging down the side of a great wave, again lurching heavily, filling the deck with water, which, as the vessel straightened up again, went dashing over to the weather-side, often out over the rail, and some of it finding its way, through the binnacle, into the cabin.

The remark of one of our boys that "any one who can't swim had better take a back seat" was certainly very apt, but the gravity of the situation, and the dangers incident to running in such a gale, with the sea on the quarter, were better expressed by the order, frequently shouted to the man at the wheel, "Watch her sharp, now! Keep your eye to wind'ard, and if you see a big one coming, swing her off and let her take it stern-to."

January 27: At 10 a.m. we passed about a half a mile to windward of a large brig-rigged steamship. She was heading to the westward and had fore and main trysails and close-reefed fore and main topsails set; was badly iced up and going slow ... At 4 p.m. a "flopper" broke over the quarter, some of which came into the cabin and wet the book in which I am writing my journal. This is a bad time for writing, but I shall not soon get a better chance.

February 1: Two of our men are on the sick list with very bad colds, and as I have to be both nurse and doctor, I am busy most of the time.

February 3: [One of his patients was still too sick to fish, so] I had to go in a dory myself this morning, and my parting injunction to all hands, as we left the side, was: "Now, boys, you all know that the glass is low, and you must make your own almanacs. If you see a squall coming, or find that it is breezing up, you'd better strike for the vessel."

Our trawl was to windward of the beam. We pulled for the outer buoy, but before we got to it a wild-looking snow squall was coming down on us like a race horse from the WSW. I thought by the looks of it that it would "make things hum" when it struck, and said to Phil Merchant, my dorymate, "I think we'd better slew around and *scatter* for the vessel. We're to windward, and are all right ourselves, but if the squall strikes as heavy as it looks, those fellows to leeward can never pull up in the world, and the best thing we can do is to get aboard as soon as we can and pay our dory down to them."

Accordingly we kept off and pulled for the vessel, but before we got far the squall was upon us. It blew smart for awhile, but there was not as much wind and snow as I had expected there would be. Three of the dories reached the side just after we did, but there were two others out, one which was dead to leeward and one to windward, the crews of which held on.

Once back aboard, Collins and Merchant paid their dory down by the buoy line to the pair to leeward and pulled them home to the *Marion*. The lads in the windward dory had to abandon part of their trawl before rowing down to the vessel. All safe on board, "one of the men is catching some kittiwake gulls for a pot pie."

February 8: It is nothing unusual while sitting in the cabin for one to look out of the companionway and see the water dripping off the end of the mainboom; for when the vessel's stern falls in the hollow of a sharp sea the end of the boom is frequently immersed to a depth of two or three feet. The cook set a short "bull-tow" (18 hooks) this afternoon and caught six fine halibut.

February 10: Ten a.m., smart SSE gale and thick snow. At 10:35 the watch sang out, "Here's a feller drifting down close to us." We were all on deck in a minute, but the first glance showed that the vessel was drifting clear of us, and with the remark, "Oh, he's all right; he'll go clear of us," the crew went below again, all except the watch and myself. I tried to make out what vessel it was, but was unable to. The weather was so thick that, although she drifted by us not more than 150 fathoms distant, I could only see the blur of her hull and spars showing indistinctly through the snow and flying spray

A little land bird (a snow bunting) came aboard this afternoon. As an evidence of the strength of wing possessed by these little creatures it is only necessary to mention that the nearest land is Cape Freels, Newfoundland, 128 miles distant.

The wind increased, and to get the best possible hold on the bottom they stuck out almost all their anchor cable. By nightfall it was a screecher from the northeast, estimated at hurricane strength by Collins, with dense snow.

We had two men in a watch, one stationed on the foregaff and the other on the main [the sails were furled, obviously], so as to be out of the way if the vessel shipped a sea. In this way the men kept the best lookout they could. But looking to windward is hardly possible in such a gale, with the snow, sleet, and spray driving furiously to leeward and nearly blinding whoever turns his face to windward. But the attempt must be made, for in such a gale there is imminent danger of some other vessels driving down across our hawse, and if these should not be seen in time for us to cut the cable, and thus prevent a collision, both would sink.

One or the other of the watch occasionally comes below to look at the clock and ascertain how the time is passing, and also to get his breath. As they brush the snow and frozen spray from their eyes, hair, and beard, they often remark, "I tell yer what 'tis, this is a tough one. If this haint a regular old-fashioned screamer I never saw one." They are, however, confident of the ability of the vessel to ride the gale out in safety, and to the question of "How does she ride?" they reply, "Ride? Why, she shames the gulls! But there's some wild seas going; some regular old tearers that give her all she can do to climb over them."

February 11: The men have been variously employed today, each to his own taste; some have been making mats out of buoy line; others patching oil-clothes, reading &c.; while one poor fellow with a penchant for card playing has been coaxing someone to play a game with him. "Anything you like," he says; "state your game, only say you'll play."

February 13: [With plenty of anchor cable out against a living gale, the *Marion* would hold it pretty taut and off the bottom. But let the wind fall off, and the cable slack . . . After being on deck most of the night, Captain Collins turned in, awoke at 10,] but not hearing the familiar roar of breaking waves, and howling of the wind, I knew at once that it had moderated. I immediately turned out and inquired of the watch how long it had been since the wind died away.

"Only about half an hour or less," he replied. "Why did you not call me before? You knew I wanted to be called if it died away," I said. "Well, I didn't know but what it'd blow agin soon; it looks nuff like it," he answered in a dogged sort of manner. It could not be denied that it did look "nuff like it," nevertheless I told him to call the men forward and we would heave in some cable, at the same time rousing out the after crowd.

We had hove in only about 30 fathoms before I knew by the bearings of the [*Edwin C.*] *Dolliver* [a nearby schooner] that we were adrift. After the cable was in we found that it was chafed off square as an ax would cut it, and that we had lost 120 fathoms. It is probable that the cable was not on the bottom more than half an hour, and it must have come in contact with a very sharp rock to cut it off so quickly . . . This is a special misfortune to us at this particular time, for the good prospects which we had of obtaining a fine fare of halibut are thus ruined in an hour, since we have not cable enough left to ride in deep water.

February 15: In the northwest the sky looked squally and unsettled. Under such circumstances I did not dare set our gear, for fear of losing it if the wind should blow up strong. Seeing the crew of the *N. H. Phillips* turning their dories over, I concluded to do the same and start with her for home. All hands were called and we swayed up the lower sails, and after having lashed the backstay outrigger to the after crosstree, so that the backstay would support the topmast and prevent it from being carried away, we set the staysail. We were astern and a little to leeward of the *Phillips* when we set the staysail, but soon caught up with her and passed to leeward of her. At noon she was nearly hull down astern.

I have rarely ever started for home feeling so much dissatisfied as now. I was confident of getting a good fare of fish this time, and am quite sure we would have succeeded in doing so if we had not lost our cable. What influenced me to start for home today — aside from the loss of our cable — is because I think we will probably reach there about the first of Lent, and may possibly get a better price for our fish at that time than if we arrive later.

February 16: We had strong puffs of wind all of last night, and at times the vessel had all she could stagger under . . . We could see the *Phillips* astern this morning. She was a little to leeward of our wake and probably about 8 or 9 miles distant. Two steamships and a sailing ship passed us this forenoon going east . . . At 11:30 p.m. the cry came down the gangway, "Hear the news there below. The main halyards have parted, and you'll have to turn out and fix 'em." All hands accordingly roused out and hauled down the mainsail. We then spliced the halyards and put a mat over the copper on the jaws of the gaff, which had worn through, and being "rucked up," cut the rope like a knife.

February 20: At 12:15 a.m. (correct apparent time) we made Thacher's Island Lights a point on the weather bow, and, as we headed, we would have just about struck Eastern Point. The wind at this time was veering easterly, with indications of snowing thick very soon, and shortly after snow began to fall, though it did not immediately get very thick. "Beautiful snow" may sound very pretty and poetical, but it certainly is not appreciated very much by one coming on the coast in winter. I was kept in a constant state of anxiety concerning the weather, as there was every appearance of a coming gale. The lights kept disappearing and reappearing as we neared them, being hidden most of the time, keeping me in suspense between hope and fear; hoping that the snow would not shut down thick before we got in, and fearing it might be so dense as to preclude all possibility of making the land until daylight, before which time it might blow a gale, and compel us to haul off.

At last Thacher's Island Lights were entirely shut in and we saw no more of them; but as it was not so thick to the westward and we had got pretty well in, a glimpse of Eastern Point Light was obtained, and we steered straight for it. The wind in the meantime had hauled out to SE, and began to breeze up smart. As the snow grew thicker and thicker we barely kept sight of the Point Light, although, with every foot of canvas spread, we were running toward it at least 9 or 10 knots an hour. We lost sight of it several times, and when passing by it I do not think we could see objects more than a half-mile distant. We anchored off Harbor Cove at 3 a.m., furled the sails and went ashore.

February 21, 1879: It blew a heavy gale from the NE last night; this morning there was still a smart breeze and some undertow heaving in the harbor, which is usually the case after an easterly gale. The "hawkers" wanted the halibut to send away, so we took a tug, which towed the vessel into the Atlantic Halibut Company's wharf. The undertow made it very difficult to lie at this wharf, the vessel surging back and forth considerably. She parted several times, and we had much trouble to hold her. Toward noon it was smoother.

We finished taking the halibut out in the afternoon, and towed down to our own

171

wharf [Sylvanus Smith Fisheries]. We weighed off, heads and all, 36,855 pounds of halibut, all in splendid condition. Fourteen per cent was deducted for the heads, for which we receive nothing. This deduction leaves the net weight 31,691 pounds. Net stock, $970.26; share of each man, $33.48.

So much for a four-week halibut trip to the Grand Bank in midwinter. The gale that Captain Collins and the *Marion* and crew barely swept in ahead of was the same that sank the thirteen Georgesmen and all hands, 143 of them.

12. THE FISHERMEN'S RACES

During the long thrash to windward, every vessel sailed on her lee rail, with deck buried to the hatches . . . The brave, laboring craft would roll under surging seas to the second and third ratlines; then would follow awful moments of suspense, as the unflinching crews, with teeth set and hands clenched, watched to see if their craft would stagger up again, or go down under her grievous load. Desperate as the chances were, not a vessel luffed or reefed, as to be the first to reef would make her the laughing stock of the town, and there was not a skipper in the fleet who would not carry away both sticks rather than be branded as a coward.

— William Hale, M.D., aboard the schooner *J. S. Steele* during "The Race It Blew," 1892.

Men went fishing on the gamble of a better trip than the last, or because they knew nothing else, or their fathers made them, or they must punish themselves, or escape from their women, or they knew not why. And they went for the hell of it, and were ducking their creditors, and loved the comradeship the way men love war. They were crazy about their schooners, no doubt of that. And they were crazy about sailing them.

A race — to fall in with the old *Helen B.* outward bound for the grounds, in a fisherman's breeze, everything flying but the cook's drawers — what in the world could touch it for plain teeth-setting, hand-clenching excitement? Nothing! "How does she ride?" skipper wanted to know. "Ride? Why, she shames the gulls!"

Many the unspoken challenge and offhand brush. "We were astern and a little to the leeward of the *Phillips* when we set the staysail, but soon caught up with her and passed to leeward of her. At noon she was nearly hull down astern."

A dozen and a half organized races amongst fishing schooners were sailed in the half century between the first in 1886 and the last in 1938. But the only genuine article, the one match run off between plain working vessels sailed by plain working fishermen — no yachty types, no ringers in the crew or at

173

the helm — in a regular fisherman's breeze, was the classic so heartily described by Dr. Hale at the beginning of the chapter.

"The Race It Blew" was sailed in a howling summer northeast gale, driving rain and fifty knots they swore, maybe more, on August 26, 1892, as the climax of Gloucester's six-day celebration of the two hundred fiftieth anniversary of its incorporation. The idea, of course, originated with none other than Captain Collins, whose head was down in Washington with the Fisheries Commission but whose heart still pounded at the thought of grasping the spokes of an A. P. Stoddart patented wheel under the trembling mainboom of the *Marion*, up to his knees in white water.

Now *that* was a race! A triangle of forty-one miles from the Eastern Point whistling buoy to a mark boat off Nahant to Davis Ledge off Minot's Light and back to Gloucester. Commodore Henry S. Hovey of the Eastern Yacht Club in Marblehead, Gloucester summer resident, put up silver trophies for the winners in two handicap classes, the big schooners over eighty-five feet on the waterline, seven of them, and three of less than eighty-five, starting a few minutes later. The event was well publicized, and forty thousand spectators were expected.

Most of the entries had been in Gloucester for several days, having their bottoms smoothed and painted and getting into racing trim. Anticipating light summer airs, Captain Tommie Bohlin had divested the *Nannie C. Bohlin*, one of the favorites, of a good bit of her ballast. Maurice Whalen, on the other hand, hailed into port in the *Harry L. Belden* with a trip of mackerel on the very eve of the race. Some say he had time to unload, some say not, but he had no chance to haul out for a bottom job.

Confounding every calculation, August 26 dawned with what Arthur Millett of the *Gloucester Times* called "almost the appearance of a hurricane," a slashing, ominous, chilly broth of rain and fog driven in from the Atlantic by a mounting gale. Perhaps the committee, huddled in the judges' boat bouncing around in the outer harbor, underestimated the dangers in the day ahead, little realizing in the absence of any kind of weather service that this soaker was indeed very possibly the backlash of an early season hurricane raging up the Atlantic from the tropics somewhere offshore.

If any of the skippers had his qualms, pride certainly prevented him from letting on. None backed out, nor did a single entrant, large or small, as he struggled through the rising seas for position at the starting gun, surrender to his better judgment and take in a reef.

And they were off! All the first leg the storm nipped at their heels. Wrote Millett: "They ran off the wind at a great pace, riding up on one sea only to dive into the other, the sea at times washing over them. The whole hulls would be at times buried in the trough, and the wind howled dismally through their rigging."

When the racers were about abreast of that bleak lump, Halfway Rock, off

Marblehead, the wind was unofficially clocked at nearly fifty knots. The whitecapped seas were mounting higher and sharper and wilder by the minute. The atmosphere was so thick with rain, scud and fog that nothing at all could be seen from land, to the bitter disappointment of the sensible lubbers along the North Shore, while those spectators foolhardy enough to attempt following the race by steamer and boat wished themselves on land, for they could barely distinguish the contestants when they could see them and were horribly seasick as well.

The mad Gloucestermen tore across the mad ocean in the general direction of the unseen mark boat off Nahant in tense bewilderment. Captain Sol Jacobs in the *Ethel B. Jacobs* had a commanding lead but miscalculated, came down on the mark too wide, had to jibe around to starboard all standing for the next leg, and as his mainsail snapped overhead across the deck with the roar of a thunderclap and took the full force of the gale from the opposite quarter, his main gaff whacked against the main rigging with such a crack that it broke in half like a twig. To save his sagging, flogging mainsail, he had to haul it down, set his riding sail in its place and limp for home, out of the race. Seeing Sol's folly, the others approached the mark with more care, but it was too much at that point for the *Grayling* and the *James S. Steele* (with Dr. Hale aboard); they quit and joined the spectators.

All the while, "the pet of the fleet," the pretty little *Lottie S. Haskins*, danced along in the lead of her smaller class to the wonderment of any who could make her out. Not long after he launched her in 1890, Mel McClain (in astonishment at his creation) had sailed the *Haskins* by the wind and wearing nothing but her staysail, as we have seen, all the way up the harbor to her berth.

One way and another the fleet that stuck with it rounded the leeward mark off Minot's Light and hit for home in the teeth of the gale. Millett: "With every sheet hauled flat and every sail drawing, they pounded and staggered into the heavy seas, burying their bowsprits and washing decks at every jump. Lee rails were buried and the water was up to the hatches as the schooners laid over before the strength of the fierce northeaster. Sea after sea they shipped and sometimes dove into them to their foremasts."

With Jacobs and his *Ethel B.* out of it, the *Belden* took over the lead. She was a new schooner, designed by Tom McManus and built in '89, a plumb-stemmer with the longest bowsprit in Gloucester and a reputation as "a slippery piece of wood." And so she was, and "almost on her beam ends," in the awed words of Arthur Millett, "the seas all the time breaking over her."

Standing in for the finish off Eastern Point, Maurice Whalen brought the *Belden* about, and as all her canvas flogged while she dove and leaped through irons, the jib tore from its sheets and in a moment had flailed to rags. The *Joseph Rowe*, close astern, lost both jibs, and, as the foresail started to go, was passed by the *Nannie C. Bohlin*, a lifeline rigged all around her deck, perilously light on ballast where her skipper had outfoxed himself.

And now the finish! "On she came standing up like a church," exulted Millett of the *Belden*, "great seas foaming under her bow and breaking over her to leeward . . . Such a shout as went up from those on the judges' boat as she crossed the line! Captain Whalen, all oiled up, stood by the wheel of his staunch craft and waved his hand gleefully in reply to the greeting."

Thirty-five years later James B. Connolly, who was not on hand but let nothing get in the way of a good story, wrote of that moment: "There was an old fisherman hanging to the weather rigging of his vessel to see the finish. As the smoke from the finish gun puffed out he leaped into the air, knocking his heels together and roaring at the brave sight of her: 'Maurice wins, he to his neck in water! The *Harry Belden* wins, the able *Harry Belden* sailin' across the line on her side an' her crew sittin' out on her keel!'"

Twelve minutes behind the *Belden* came the *Nannie C.*, "all slick and shiny, looking very yachty as she glided through the water . . . her lee rail buried from view and the water rushing over her deck." So Millett viewed her. Next was the *Joseph Rowe,* headsails in rags, four minutes behind the *Bohlin.* And thirty minutes later in comes the *Lottie Haskins* out of the thick, gallant as could be, and the diminutive *Caviare*, forty more behind *her*, both of them with reefed foresails, followed somewhere back there by the *Elsie F. Rowe,* which fought gamely before dropping out.

Connolly it was who plucked from this race the colorful and daring Tommie Bohlin and his *Nannie C.* as the models for his hero and heroine of many a yarn, Tommie Ohlsen and the *Nannie O.* And it was Jim Connolly, rest his good Celtic soul, who must shoulder the responsibility for the grandest figment of Apocrypha to emerge from a race that needed no hyperbole in the retelling: namely, that Whalen, Bohlin and Jacobs ordered their halyards lashed aloft at the start so that "if any timid crew member tried that day to let any main halyards run [to drop the sail and spill the wind and save her from capsizing], he would have to go aloft to do it, and before he could get aloft he would be headed off."

Halyards lashed aloft or not, "The Race It Blew" (as coined by Connolly) was *the* bona fide fishermen's race, the daftest and the greatest of them all. And the wisest comment, when he (and his stomach) had calmed down somewhat the next day back in the office of the *Gloucester Times*, was delivered by Arthur Millett: "The boats all had too much sail on, and it was playing to the galleries to carry it. All would have sailed faster under reefs."

For all its madness, the tempestuous mayhem perpetrated off the North Shore by the grizzled Gloucestermen on August 26, 1892, did serve some redeeming social purpose. It was not the first but the third such vulgarian antidote of the common man in his dirty oilskins to the series of genteel donnybrooks for the America's Cup staged off Sandy Hook during those years of international amity between the millionaires of the defending former colonies and forever challenging Britain, in their blazers and brass buttons. "The vessels certainly were getting ready to start in conditions never before seen by the writer," marveled one of the country's leading yachting scribes, who had covered every important match for twenty-five years and was on hand in his chartered tug. Even he could not contain his nauseous admiration. "It is doubtful if ever a race was sailed under such savage conditions."

The first of these proletarian postscripts had been dashed off by the fishermen in May of 1886, following as night on day the successful defense of the America's Cup the previous September by the sloop *Puritan*, designed by Boston's native genius of beam and draft, Edward Burgess. The organizer was the youthful Tom McManus, himself a promising local designer of fishing schooners, and the first across the finish in Boston Bay were the *John H. McManus*, named for his father, sailmaker for the Boston Cup defenders, and the pilot schooner *Hesper*, the creations of Dennison J. Lawlor, Boston designer-builder. Little wind and a dull affair.

The same year, '86, Burgess's *Mayflower* won the honor of beating back the British. The next, '87, his *Volunteer* made it three in a row for him, and the year after that, in the spring of 1888, his first venture into the design of working schooners, the brand-new and marvelously swift *Carrie I. Phillips*, won the second fishermen's race.

Others of the new breed of deeper, safer, faster schooners that were springing from the drawing boards of Lawlor, Burgess, McClain and McManus in response to the campaigning of Joseph Collins were tested and showed their stuff in these first two meetings of the fishermen, compromised as they were by yachtsmen's conditions. So it was with reason that Collins proposed the great race of '92 "in view of the excellence that has been attained in recent years in the construction and rig of fishing vessels . . . and the superior skill of our fishermen in managing them."

Before the First World War put a stop to such good times two more fishermen's races were sponsored more or less as publicity for their sponsors. The first was the inspiration of Thomas W. Lawson, the flamboyant Boston financial manipulator, run off in September 1901, a few weeks before *Columbia*'s defense of the America's Cup, and won by a Boston vessel. Next year he underwrote in his own honor the only seven-masted schooner ever thus vaingloriously contrived.

The second, a listless show, came off in 1907 at the behest of Sir Thomas Lipton, the Scottish-born Irish tea king, who happened to be between challenges for The Auld Mug with one or another of his *Shamrock*s and was interested in keeping his benignly goateed countenance before the sipping public. A Provincetown boat made off with the Lipton Cup.

By World War I it was plain to all but the hopelessly nostalgic that power was pushing into the fisheries, sail was drifting out. In 1900 the King of the

Mackerel Killers, Sol Jacobs, had built the *Helen Miller Gould*, the first large fishing schooner to be equipped with a gasoline auxiliary engine, and in 1902 the *Alice M. Jacobs,* the first big fishing steamer. In 1905 Boston parties launched the *Spray*, the first American otter trawler, an idea borrowed from the English. *Spray* was the pioneer dragger, pulling across the bottom the wide-mawed net that would revolutionize deep-sea fishing and put into motion the apparently irreversible hauldown of sail.

But there was life in the old breed yet. And fight in old Lipton, too. In 1920, after seventeen years of counting his tea bags, Sir Thomas bid for the fourth time, with *Shamrock IV*, whose 1914 challenge had been postponed by the war. The New York Yacht Club responded with *Resolute*, from the Wizard of Bristol, Nathanael Herreshoff. That July off Sandy Hook the challenger took one race when *Resolute* had a rigging problem — the only win against seventeen losses endured by Lipton's *Shamrock*s in his thirty-two-year quest for the ever-elusive Mug.

The more significant race of that 1920 series, however, was the one called off because of rough seas. Shades of '92. Such chickenheartedness was too much for the publisher of the *Halifax Herald and Mail*, William H. Dennis, who regarded with disgust the spectacle of the Mother Country, once Queen of the Oceans, harbor-bound by a little wind.

No *Canadian* would be bothered by a bit of a breeze, the *Herald* snorted — not a salt banker from Lunenburg, down on the south shore of Nova Scotia where the heft of the fishing fleet hailed from, not a *Bluenose*. And so, that very October, the newspaper flung out a challenge for an international fishermen's championship of the North Atlantic (directed at Gloucester, Massachusetts; where else?), a race for *real* sailors, for $5000 and a handsome silver cup.

Immediately the *Gloucester Times* and the Gorton-Pew Fisheries picked up the gauntlet. Gorton's sent Captain Marty Welch and its *Esperanto*, which happened to be in port, to Halifax, where she roundly beat the Lunenburger *Delawana* two straight and sailed back to a crowing Gloucester with the prize in early November.

Thus good-naturedly enough commenced the nineteen-year racing rivalry between Gloucester and Lunenburg, the United States and Canada. Except that for a couple of centuries the Canadians had endured the larceny of their mackerel and their herring at the hands of invading Americans, and of their best fishermen enticed by the U.S. dollar to Gloucester — and now, from under their blue noses, the grand larceny of what one and all had been so sure was to be their very own for keeps, a Canada's Cup!

Outrage led to action, and action to counteraction. *Esperanto* had hardly cleared Halifax with the silver when a Nova Scotian syndicate headed by Captain Angus Walters of Lunenburg had the Canadian designer William J.

1

1. Preparing to do business in great waters, some schooners of Gloucester await orders and a breeze at the head of Harbor Cove around 1907. (Ernest L. Blatchford, Thomas Collection)

2. The child is the father of the man. Halibut come out at the New England Fish Company eighty years ago, and either it is after school or the truant officer is elsewhere. The tug *Eveleth* lies on the outside of the Boston and Gloucester steamship wharf. Manager Blatchford's office is in the far corner of the building, and not much happens outside his window that he isn't there to snap. (Ernest L. Blatchford, Thomas Collection)

2

1. Winter on the banks. The helmsman of the *Onato*, around 1905. (Chester L. Morrissey)

2. Front Street remains choked with snow two days after the blizzard of April 3, 1861 in what may be the earliest surviving photograph of Gloucester. Three years later a February fire, starting here in the West End and fanned by a gale, roared through 103 buildings on the waterfront before it was stopped. Front was renamed Main when Rogers Street was built on the ashes above the wharves. (Author's Collection)

3. Captain Joseph W. Collins. (*Cape Ann Advertiser*)

4. *Marion* was only two years old when Captain Collins took her halibuting in January of 1879. She is depicted here at anchor on the grounds under her steadying sail. The men are baiting up. The cook shakes out a tablecloth up forward, and the skipper stands by at the quarter with his speaking trumpet to hail the approaching schooner. Neil Johnson and Charles Culvert were drowned when their dory capsized fishing from *Marion* in June of 1877, a few weeks after she was launched. John Higgins and David McDonald were lost in their dory in the fog when they were separated from *Marion* on Western Bank on March 28, 1880. (Goode's *Fisheries*)

1

2   3

4

1, 2. January of 1875 was a bad, bitterly cold and blowy month on land and sea. The Gloucester schooners *David Burnham* and *Joseph Chandler* and twenty-four men were lost on the banks. February started out no better. The deepest freeze in decades struck and gripped the coast. By the end of the first week Gloucester Harbor was frozen solid out beyond Dog Bar buoy off the end of Eastern Point. Fifty Georgesmen all ready to sail were immobilized by what the *Cape Ann Advertiser* dubbed the "ice embargo." Local towboats strove, mostly unsuccessfully, to keep a semblance of a partial channel open, and a tug was chartered from Boston to help. People tramped out across the harbor to Ten Pound Island and on as far as Black Bess Point on Eastern Point. Gangs of fishermen, their livelihood depending on getting out, tried to cut channels through the ice for their vessels. Baiters delivered herring to the impatient schooners in pungs drawn across the ice by teams of men, even in dories with makeshift runners.

One day the *Fitz J. Babson* labored in from sea, iced-up worse than any of the greybeards had ever seen — thick as a stovepipe, they said, on her standing rigging. Coming on the coast from the banks, the crew had been up all night beating off ice just to keep afloat.

It thawed momentarily during the second week in February, poured rain and froze again, making the harbor ice as smooth as glass. Hundreds came out to skate, came out in their sleighs, even in ox carts, or whizzed around in ice boats. And the tinkerers built runners under their dories, raised mast and sail, and soared off.

The schooner *T. L. Mayo*, Captain Vibert, had sailed from La Have Bank on January 22 with 9,000 pounds of halibut and 42,000 of codfish, reporting very cold and rough weather. But the *Mayo* got top dollar for the halibut, refitted for Georges Bank under Captain Nickerson and sailed just ahead of the freeze-up. On February 15 the *T. L. Mayo* and the *G. W. Stetson* returned in company from Georges, both heavily iced-up, poked their way in as far as they could and got frozen in solid. The *Mayo* had broken her windlass under the tremendous strain of the surging seas, so that they couldn't raise anchor and has to cut the cable and lose everything outside the hawse pipe. On the *Stetson*, at the worst of it, they cut and lost their anchor and 250 fathoms of brand new cable to avoid being drifted down on by the *Hattie B. West* of Gloucester, which had broken loose.

Two more of Gloucester's schooners took twenty-four more men to the bottom that week, the *Sarah H. Cressy* and the *J. C. Call*, while of the Nova Scotian coast the *William H. Thurston* was lost, the crew providentially saved.

The photographer set up his stereoscopic camera on the steamboat wharf when the ice was at its worst that February of 1875, looking across the Georgesmen, and got the towboat *Camilla* valiantly attempting what naught but nature finally accomplished.

Turning his camera in the other direction, he photographed the *T. L. Mayo*, the one with the two blurred figures in the stern (a time exposure being necessary). The *G. W. Stetson* is probably one of the nearer vessels. The *Mayo*'s entire cabin top is gone, suggesting that the owners decided to repair the cabin along with the windlass while they were at it, and ice-bound anyway. (Thomas Collection)

1

2

3

_1._ Captain Collins had to use very little imagination when he collaborated with artist H.W. Elliott to show a heavily iced-up Gloucesterman riding out a gale at anchor on the Grand Bank a hundred years ago. (Goode's _Fisheries_)

_2._ "A Struggle for Life," Captain Collins hand-captioned this graphic sketch from all-too-vivid memory; "Caught to leeward in a squall." A trawl buoy has been drifted downwind of the schooner, and the dorymates are rowing for it, and for dear life. Fifty-two dorymen went astray from Gloucester vessels and were lost in two months of the spring of 1883 alone. (Goode's _Fisheries_)

_3._ An unidentified schooner heaves home to Gloucester, logey with ice. "Sometimes, for days and nights together," wrote Captain Collins, "the men must remain on deck, constantly employed in pounding the ice and always at the imminent risk of being swept overboard. Vessels sometimes arrive in fishing ports so badly iced up that it is impossible to lower the sails or to bring them to anchor." Freezing spray, according to _The Fishermen's Own Book_, "in a bitter cold day hardens as soon as it strikes, and piles itself up on the overburdened craft with amazing quickness. Then the safety of the vessel and her management through the cold, seething waters, render it an imperative necessity that the ice be dislodged, and a cold, cheerless task it is which the fisherman has forced upon him. Short spells of this ice pounding, with the temperature below zero, is all that men can endure, and they are frequently relieved, all hands taking their turn and making the best of an unwelcome duty." More than one Gloucesterman foundered and sank under the burden. The schooners most especially made ice coming on the coast in the face of a stiffening offshore nor'wester. Fishing off the Canadian Maritimes, they sometimes limped into Nova Scotian ports to get the ice steamed off. (Frank Shute Collection, Cape Ann Historical Association)

185

186

3

🕊 *1, 2.* Lucky — and unlucky — was the *Cavalier*, being towed back to Gloucester by the Coast Guard Cutter *Androscoggin* on February 23, 1911. Her flag is at half-mast for Nova Scotian dorymates Tom Babine and Jack Porper, who went astray from her trawling for halibut on the Grand Bank January 25. That was the Novies' and *Cavalier's* bad luck. Her good luck — if it could be called that — came a few days later when she made sail for Gloucester with a full fare of halibut and was overtaken by a fresh norther of such strength that Captain Bob Porper, a cousin of Jack, decided to take in the mainsail. As the riding sail was being bent on something gave way — perhaps the bobstay from the end of the bowsprit to the stem at the waterline — and with a horrible, splintering crash everything came down — bowsprit, foremast, main topmast and all the rigging and sails. The luck of it was that no one was hurt, let alone killed. They got up a jury rig and set sail for Gloucester again, only to be blown three hundred miles east southeast of Cape Ann, where the *Androscoggin* spotted their distress signal (no radio in those days) and took *Cavalier* in tow. Hundreds came down for a look at the gallant cripple at the wharf of the New England Fish Company, where omnipresent amateur photographer Blatchford was the manager. (Ernest L. Blatchford, Thomas Collection)

🕊 *3.* Gloucester Harbor is no teapot in a tempest, and was never less so than in all the years before the breakwater was finally finished off Eastern Point in 1905. The great gale of December 15, 1839 wrecked twenty schooners on the western shore, dismasted thirty more at anchor; an unknown number of lives were lost. The storm of February 1, 1898 drove twenty-five vessels ashore and caused the loss of at least twenty lives. For the fishermen, it was drowning in the bathtub. That November 26 the infamous blizzard of hurricane force that sank the steamer *Portland* with 157 aboard — the Portland Breeze — paralyzed Cape Ann under snow and wrecked twenty-seven vessels and forty small yachts in Gloucester Harbor alone. Miraculously, not a life was lost. Hardly had the wreckage been cleared when yet a third blizzard struck on February 13, 1899. Among the casualties was the *Elsie M. Smith*, just back from Newfoundland with frozen herring for bait. She was swept from the anchorage up on the snowy west shore of Rocky Neck, nose down, rear ignominiously in the air. After taking off some herring, they floated her and towed her over to Burnham's railways for repairs. (Ernest L. Blatchford, Thomas Collection)

187

Lifesaving drill for the volunteer crew of the Massachusetts Humane Society's Station 7 at Cressy's Beach on the western shore of Gloucester Harbor in 1902, in the wake of the havoc of '98 and '99, was serious business. The Lyle gun has fired the projectile carrying the light whip line over to the "wreck," an anchored coasting schooner. The sailors have hauled in the whip, then the hawser, and made the block fast to the foremasthead. The land end, hiked above the imaginary surf on portable shears, has been secured with the sand anchor, the breeches buoy sent out by the pulley, and the first of the "rescued" is on his way aloft and ashore before the appreciative crowd. In the distance is the line of Eastern Point and the half-finished granite breakwater. In 1902 the station was taken over by the U.S. Life-Saving Service and moved a mile south to Dolliver's Neck. The photograph was taken by the well-known Gloucester artist, A.W. Buhler. (Dorothy Buhler)

Thirteen was doubly unlucky for the *Elsie M. Smith*. Three years to the very night after she drove ashore on Rocky Neck, on February 13, 1902, she got caught in a northeast snowstorm, lost her position and was hove up over the outer bar and onto Orleans Beach at the elbow of Cape Cod with ten thousand pounds of fish. Pounding seas opened her seams and she filled. Most of the crew of eighteen took to the rigging, but a few panicked, ignoring the orders of Captain Nickerson, and launched a dory, which got away from them. A second smashed alongside. A third was put over, and two men leaped in. It capsized, and by some blind luck they were washed ashore alive. A fourth dory was swung over and three more jumped in. A giant comber picked it up and pitched it over. One of the occupants made it to the beach; the other two drowned. Meanwhile the *Elsie M. Smith* had been spotted by a patrol from the Old Harbor Life-Saving Station, who fired off a flare that brought crews from both the Old Harbor and Orleans stations. They set up the gun, fired out the projectile and line, and one by one the remaining thirteen came ashore over the raging surf by breeches buoy. "Had the entire crew patiently remained on board the schooner until the arrival of the life-savers," chided the report of the U.S. Life-Saving Service, predecessor of the Coast Guard, "none would have been lost, and on the other hand had there been no life-saving station in the vicinity, all as they themselves testify, must have frozen to death in the rigging, or, if they had drifted ashore, miserably perished on the bleak, midwinter sands." (The Mariners' Museum)

189

2

1. June in January. Fresh in from a battle with the elements, the big schooner *Oriole* lies at Jordan's wharf on January 27, 1911, proclaiming with patriotic if somewhat tattered flamboyance the nuptials of the firm's treasurer, Orlando Merchant. The *Avalon* is tied up outside. *Oriole* was one of the giants of the fleet, 127 feet overall, designed by McManus and built in 1908 by Tarr and James. She carried a great spread of canvas, and it was claimed hit sixteen knots once, notably faster than she was designed for. Sadly, *Oriole* was rammed and sunk by the Norwegian steamer *Borghild* in a dense fog off Nova Scotia on August 12, 1916, with loss of four crew. (Chester N. Walen, Thomas Collection)

2. The boisterous bard from South Boston, author of many the Gloucester fishing yarn, James B. Connolly, and Captain Martin Welch at the wheel of the gallant but outclassed schooner *Elsie* during the 1921 races with the Canadian challenger *Bluenose* off Halifax. *Bluenose* was twenty-five feet longer and eleven years younger — and she was masterfully sailed. The previous year Marty and *Esperanto* took the international cup in the one and only official Yankee victory of the eighteen-year series. (Thomas Collection)

1

1. The hopes of Gloucester slide into the Essex River with beautiful *Columbia*. It is noon on April 17, 1923 at the yard of Arthur D. Story. (The Mariners' Museum)

2. Perched like birds on the crosstrees, *Columbia*'s mastheadmen have one hand for the job and one for themselves during the elimination race off Gloucester on October 21, 1923, when the Gem of the Ocean beat the *Henry Ford* and *Elizabeth Howard* for the crack at the *Bluenose*. *Columbia* spreads 9,300 square feet of sail. The foretopmast at right is forty-two feet long, five less than the main top where Jack Sparrow holds sway at the hounds. The job of the mastheadman is to unfurl the gaff topsails so they can be set by the halyards from the deck. The foremastheadman in addition has to carry the tack and clew of the foretopsail up and over the maintopmast stay (between the maintopmasthead and the foremast cap) when *Columbia* comes about on the other tack, else there will be hell to pay if the fore gaff swings over and the topsail jams against both the maintopmast stay and the triatic, or spring stay, between the fore and main mast caps. The stays are crucial to the integrity of the schooner's whole rig, especially when these "kites" are flying, and present yet another challenge: the vast fisherman's staysail, that can be seen as a backdrop behind the foresail and fore gafftopsail, has to be lowered to the deck while the vessel is in stays between tacks; the halyards must be switched with lightning speed before it is raised again on the new lee side of the triatic and the counterstay, which runs from the foretopmasthead to the main cap. Complicated, tacking and jibing a Gloucesterman in full dress, and a good stiff breeze, and a sea running, requiring steel nerves and near-perfect precision on deck and aloft. And the outcome of a close race could depend on it. (Courtesy of E.S. Bosley, Thomas Collection)

3. The sometimes friendly rivals, Captain Ben Pine of *Columbia* and Captain Angus Walters of *Bluenose*, aboard *Columbia* at Halifax October 30, 1923, the day after Angus beat Ben in the first race by one minute and twenty seconds. (Thomas Collection)

2

3

🦅 *Columbia* swashbuckles by with the surging drive of what many cherished as the greatest of the Gloucestermen. A reaching breeze off Cape Ann, plenty enough for the maintopsail and balloner — no call to raise the half-doused foretopsail any higher or the staysail crumpled on deck. Laying back on the spreader, the mainmastheadman waves his cap in pure exuberance to Adolph Kupsinel, Gloucester professional photographer who has his hands full changing glass plate negatives in time to catch his galloping subject. Thirteen, fifteen, or even the fabled seventeen knots Jim Connolly claimed for *Columbia* one day? Not quite, but boiling along for sure. (Adolph Kupsinel)

Last of the Gloucester schooners, the *Gertrude L. Thebaud* floats high without ballast and spars in the Essex River a few minutes after smoking down Arthur D. Story's ways on March 17, 1930. Leslie Jones, ubiquitous photographic chronicler of his times for the *Boston Herald*, crouched in the "skeleton," as he put it, of another vessel abuilding to snap the tug *Eveleth* getting a line aboard for the tow around to Gloucester and Piney's Atlantic Supply Company wharf for fit-out. (Leslie Jones)

1. Broad-reaching, the *Thebaud* knifes through the sea, her bow the picture of the pure power of sail. (Adolph Kupsinel)

2. A close one in the last of the fishermen's races, October 1938 off Gloucester. The *Thebaud*'s main boom, seventy-one feet long, just squeaks by *Bluenose*'s starboard fore rigging. A foul would have lost the race then and there. Note the outboard details of the *Thebaud*'s main topping lift. (Courtesy of E.S. Bosley, Thomas Collection)

3. Thebaud leaves the smooth, foam-flecked wake that's the sure sign of an inspired design, so easy on her helm that Ben Pine requires only one hand to steer by. (Courtesy of E.S. Bosley, Thomas Collection)

2

3

1

🕊 *1.* Helpless racers on a windless sea. The *Gertrude L. Thebaud* picks up a tow back to Gloucester as the second race of the '38 series is called off on October 12. The magnificent *Bluenose* awaits her tug. (The Associated Press, Thomas Collection)

🦅 *2.* Albert Cook Church, the inspired New Bedford marine photographer, was aboard the *Thebaud* for her trials against the indomitable but ever outclassed *Elsie* off Gloucester in October 1931, prelude to the Halifax series that year with its usual outcome against *Bluenose*. Ben Pine was not well, and his racing mate, the veteran Captain John Matheson, had the helm most of the time. Church catches lanky John in solitary command at the wheel — cap, necktie, waistcoat, gold watch chain, cigar and boots. The main sheet leads from a double block on deck behind the wheelbox to a triple block on the boom three times and back through a fairlead to belay on one or the other of the quarter bitts; it is three and a half inches in circumference and must be close to four hundred feet long. (Albert Cook Church, The Whaling Museum)

Seventy feet above deck the *Thebaud*'s foremastheadman, perhaps John Hackett, hangs on with an arm, a hand and both feet. The staysail luffs at the foot, in spite of the fact that the burgee at the topmasthead flies almost abeam, suggesting that the clew down off camera to the right needs sheeting in. Occasionally, when running before the wind, the racing fishermen would "scandalize" the staysail — setting it upside down as a spinnaker opposing the foresail. The giant young adventurer and movie actor-to-be, Sterling Hayden, played the mainmasthead to Jack Hackett's foremast in the 1938 races, swinging and swaying and pitching and whipping exponentially to the slightest motion of the hull so far below. Hackett yelled across at him, as Hayden recalled in his book *Wanderer*: "Oh dyin' Jaysus, boy, if she catches one o' them seas just right she'll pitch us clean to New-found-land!" An incredulous few still remember Hayden crossing from one masthead to the other, hand over hand along the thirty feet of springstay. (Albert Cook Church, The Whaling Museum)

200

Drive 'er, boys! A man could get washed overboard down on the lee side hauling the headsail sheets. (Albert Cook Church, The Whaling Museum)

1

202

2

1. Off the wind and sheets well started, the *Gertrude L. Thebaud* swishes along through her own suds. Some of the crew and a guest or two take the shade at the break in the deck. The tackle running from a block just ahead of the main sheet (similarly shackled this side of the foresheet in the foreground) to the block hooked to the boom near the mast is the boom guy. When running in a seaway, the forward blocks of both the main and fore guys may be hooked to heavy iron staples on the rails aft of the shrouds, and the tackles belayed. The point is to hold the booms outboard when she's rolling and to keep the sails full. (Albert Cook Church, The Whaling Museum)

2. John Matheson has turned over the wheel, possibly to Ben Pine, while he goes forward to check something at the lee rigging. That, in any event, is where the female guests are taking shelter from the zephyrs of autumn. (Albert Cook Church, The Whaling Museum)

1

2

1. Charging to windward with all sheets hauled, the *Thebaud* roars across the sea like an express train as the gang shifts up on the dry side, 1930s. Every one of them a seasoned skipper in his own right, they're the rear guard of the old-time sailing Gloucester fishermen. (Adolph Kupsinel)

2. Queen of the fleet and last of the all-sail Gloucester fishing schooners, the *Gertrude L. Thebaud* flies her skirts off Eastern Point. (Adolph Kupsinel)

2

🕊 1. The *Thebaud* hits a smasher on the nose, such a dive as to take the wind momentarily out of the jib. (Peabody Museum of Salem)

🕊 2. With breeze enough to satisfy the saltiest aboard, the *Gertrude L. Thebaud* crashes through the swells under her lowers only. Leslie Jones of the *Boston Herald* was on a Navy destroyer off Gloucester. (Leslie Jones, Peabody Museum of Salem)

208

🐦 *1.* Among the very few Gloucestermen that have refused to die is the auxiliary *Adventure*, built for Captain Jeff Thomas by Everett James at Essex in 1926 and named by the owner's son, Gordon. In 1934, her skipper collapsed and died aboard her after chopping ice from the rigging at sea. Captain Leo Hynes took *Adventure* for nineteen more years of dory-trawling before she was retired from fishing in 1954 — two decades during which he figured she stocked close to three and a half million dollars — likely an all-time record. (Thomas Collection)

🐦 *2.* For her second career, *Adventure* was sold into the Maine windjamming trade. Her engine was taken out and she was converted to passenger accommodations. Captain Jim Sharp bought her in 1964, painted her white, gave her back her longer spars and a maintopmast and took fifty passengers on week-long summer cruises along the Maine coast until 1988, when he donated her to The Gloucester Adventure, Inc., a non-profit group organized to operate her as an educational tall ship. Designated a National Historic Landmark, *Adventure* is under restoration. (Jim Sharp)

🐦 3. Some went the way of the incomparable *Ingomar* of the frontispiece. They were converted to auxiliaries, they were corrupted with wheelhouses, they were stripped of their wings, and were lost at sea or wrecked ashore, as *Ingomar* was on Plum Island thirty-two years later in February 1936. (Arthur Hansen, Thomas Collection)

⚓ How many, like the handsome *Claudia,* died rotting in the dock? In *Claudia*'s case the more ironic, for she lies in all that's left of Vincent's Cove in 1939, waiting to be broken up by the W.P.A. almost exactly on the spot where she was launched by John Bishop thirty-seven years earlier. (The Mariners' Museum)

Roue working on a giant of a schooner intended to be fast enough to restore national pride while getting in under the main provisions of the *Herald*'s Deed of Gift, namely, that the contestants must be working fishing schooners under 145 feet from stem to stern and 112 on the waterline. *Bluenose*, the magnificent result, was launched at Lunenburg in March 1921. She was 143 feet long and exactly 112 on the waterline, where it counted, with not an inch to spare.

The hitch was that simultaneously, in a bid of their own, a group of Bostonians had commissioned W. Starling Burgess, Edward's son and quite as brilliant in his own right, to come up with an American contender. *Mayflower*, named for his father's cup champion of '86, was launched from the James yard in Essex just two weeks after *Bluenose* and just a shade bigger. Both schooners went fishing that season. *Mayflower* showed her stern to every vessel she fell in with and raised up such jitters in both Lunenburg and Gloucester that the international race committee disqualified her as too "yachty," though she was surely as much a fisherman, for all that, as her rival.

Were the sneakered ones preempting the Gloucestermen in these twilight years of working sail? The forty-one-foot schooner *Malabar I*, sire of a dynasty of miniature fishermen beloved by generations of New England cruising yachtsmen, was launched this same year of 1921 by John G. Alden, the Boston designer who took his inspiration from the Gloucester types, one of which, *Tartar*, he had lined off while working for Bowdoin Crowninshield.

With *Mayflower* out of the running, and *Esperanto*, the presumed defender, wrecked off Sable Island that spring, there was a brief boom early in October in Gloucester for the very speedy *Arethusa*, a McManus design bought in April with his happily ill-gotten gains by that most colorful of the early Prohibition Robin Hoods, Captain Bill McCoy, and converted into a rumrunner, alias *Tomaka*. Alas, *Arethusa* née *Tomaka* was disqualified as being even less the real McCoy than *Mayflower*.

It was left for *Elsie*, another trim McManus schooner of only 124 feet, all of eleven years old, to win the American elimination, with Marty Welch again at the helm. Later that October he sailed *Elsie* with a picked crew of fishing captains to Halifax, where she lost, fighting all the way, to the overwhelmingly bigger and faster *Bluenose* and a jubilant deckload of Bluenoses.

Elsie was the last genuine working fishing schooner, designed simply as such, to compete for the international trophy. With her defeat and the disqualification of *Mayflower* the series became infected with an increasing rancor from which it never recovered. The next eighteen years saw one futile attempt after another by Gloucester, with the help of a few yachtsmen, some of the best designers in America and all the sea wisdom the old port could muster — and against a contrary fate, a plain jinx, many

211

called it — to get the cup back from the great *Bluenose* and her abrasively competitive skipper, the master helmsman Angus Walters.

Four working-racing schooners Gloucester built in the vain hope of recapturing the championship. The *Henry Ford*, 139 feet, designed by Tom McManus, and *Puritan*, 138 feet, by Starling Burgess, were built by the Story and James yards, respectively, in Essex and launched in the spring of 1922. *Columbia*, 141 feet, designed by Burgess along the lines of *Puritan*, was built by Arthur D. Story in 1923, the last all-sail Gloucester schooner. The *Gertrude L. Thebaud*, 132 feet, designed by Frank C. Paine and built by Story in 1930, was the last of them all.

Puritan was the great hope — the greatest, many said — leaving even *Mayflower* in her wake, once knocking off fifteen knots, so the press claimed. On her third fishing trip, under Captain Jeff Thomas, a co-owner, when she was less than three months old, superswift *Puritan* overran her course by some twenty miles in a dense fog one June evening and destroyed herself on Sable Island bar off the tip of Nova Scotia, with the loss of one man.

That October of 1922, off Gloucester, Captain Clayton Morrissey's *Henry Ford* gave *Bluenose* a good run in an acrimonious series marred by false starts, a protest that the *Ford*'s mainsail was too big and threats by Clayt and his men to quit. *Bluenose* finally won, not much handicapped by Angus's rare sportsmanship in shortening sail when the *Ford*'s foretopmast broke.

Columbia was next, commissioned by a Gloucester syndicate led by Captain Benjamin Pine, a native Newfoundlander. She was *fast*! Walked away from the *Henry Ford* and *Elizabeth Howard* in the trials off Gloucester. Off Halifax, that October of '23, *Columbia* lost the first race to *Bluenose* by one minute over a forty-mile course. The second was called on account of insufficient wind, but *Bluenose* had already rounded a buoy on the wrong side and the committee gave it to the Gloucesterman. Next day *Bluenose* won by two minutes. Walters refused to sail a play-off. Piney refused the trophy, and it was placed under trusteeship.

Feelings still ran high in 1926 when *Columbia* and *Bluenose* won their respective trials over the *Henry Ford* and the *Haligonian*, and when Ben Pine insisted the series be sailed in Gloucester, which had raised most of the money that year, Angus swore he would never again race anywhere but Halifax, and that was that.

While on a fishing trip on August 26, 1927, thirty-five years to the day after the great race of 1892, *Columbia* the gem went to the bottom of the ocean — no one survived to tell how — off Sable Island in a storm that also took four Lunenburg schooners. Her Nova Scotian crew of twenty-two went down with her. There were no thoughts of racing in either port that year or the next, and although trials were held at Gloucester and Lunenburg in 1929, *Bluenose* did not compete, and that again was that.

212

As he had been way back in 1907 with his trophy and in 1920 with his *Shamrock IV*, the aging Sir Thomas Lipton was responsible for the revival of the races in 1930 with his final try for the America's Cup after a lapse of ten years. *Shamrock V*, first of those dinosaurs of sailing capitalism, the skyscraping Marconi-rigged J-class sloops, was his challenge to Starling Burgess's *Enterprise*, and of course *Shamrock* lost, three in a row, off Newport in mid-September.

Financed principally by Louis Thebaud, a Gloucester summer visitor, named for his wife and managed by Ben Pine, the *Gertrude L. Thebaud* had been launched in March in anticipation of a good go with *Bluenose* for a trophy offered by Sir Thomas, the series to be sailed off Eastern Point three weeks after the battle of the J-boats. And a fitting, even overshadowing sequel, for these biggest sloops ever built were almost exactly the same length overall as the racing fishermen and carried about seventy-five hundred square feet of sail, contrasted with *Bluenose*'s more than ten thousand. As a matter of some irony, the *Thebaud*'s designer, Frank Paine, had the second-best of both worlds; he was simultaneously responsible for one of the Js, *Yankee*, eliminated in the trials by the inventive Starling Burgess's *Enterprise*.

Angus Walters was persuaded to relent on his threat never again to race out of Gloucester — and regretted it. *Bluenose* sailed up and, lo and behold, was roundly beaten by the old fox, Ben Pine, at the wheel of this new upstart *Thebaud* in the first race, and in the ill Piney's absence by Captain Charlie Johnson in the second. Angus had a ready alibi that his vessel had bumped on Round Rock Shoal at the entrance to Gloucester Harbor three times while a Gloucesterman, who chanced to be aboard, had the wheel. The second Lipton Cup remained in Gloucester, nevertheless, and its donor, the personification of international sportsmanship for thirty-two years, died the next year at the age of eighty-one.

The *Gertrude L. Thebaud*'s defeat of *Bluenose*, even though not for the *Halifax Herald* trophy, revived interest in the international races, and in 1931, after eliminating old *Elsie* in trials at Gloucester, the *Thebaud* sailed to Halifax in October under Captain John Matheson. It was hardly a contest in her home waters; *Bluenose* beat the *Thebaud* two straight.

The heavy hand of the Depression descended upon the fisheries as upon everything else, and neither vessel prospered. In 1933 the *Thebaud* sailed down to Washington, and the crew lunched with the Roosevelts in the White House to publicize the plight of the fishermen. Later that year the *Thebaud* was joined by the *Bluenose* at the Chicago World's Fair.

As the world moved toward another war in 1937, the racing fever struck — a fever more of fantasy evoked by the making of Kipling's novel into the motion picture *Captains Courageous*, which stirred the cockles of old sailing hearts in Gloucester, and by the running of the last of the three dramatic J-boat series, this time between Tom Sopwith's *Endeavour II* and Harold Vanderbilt's *Ranger* for an America's Cup that would not again be at stake for another twenty-one years.

And so the Depression year of '38 dragged around, and there must be one more fishermen's race between the guardedly friendly old enemies, Angus and Piney, who had first crossed tacks fifteen years earlier. And what a hullabaloo! For the benefit of the spectators the course was twice around an eighteen-mile triangle outside Boston Harbor — a damn merry-go-round not fit for fishermen, grumbled Captain Walters, more dyspeptic than ever, struggling with an old boat hogged in the middle from a long life fishing and trading and racing, her gear giving way when least expected.

The *Thebaud* took the first race on October 9, and *Bluenose* the second on the thirteenth. Then there were fogs and calms, and Ben Pine, ailing, turned her over to Captain Cecil Moulton, but she took longer than the time limit to beat *Bluenose* in a drifting match, and it was ruled no race. Angus snuck out some ballast to lighten her up, rather contrary to the regulations, and beat *Thebaud* for the second time on October 23 when the committee decided to look the other way. The next day Gloucester came back and beat Lunenburg to even the score when *Bluenose*, leading, parted a topmast stay.

On October 26, 1938, *Bluenose* won her last race, the last fishermen's race, slipping across the finish just two minutes and fifty seconds ahead of her most dogged challenger, in the usual cloud of recriminations.

That was the final gasp of even the appearance of fishing under sail, which had really been moribund for twenty-five years. World War II finished off all the old ways. *Bluenose* wound up in the Caribbean trade and was wrecked off Haiti in 1946. The *Gertrude L. Thebaud* smashed her bones not far away, on the coast of Venezuela, two years later.

It was a new world after the First War, and not so brave a one at that. More and more, the races after 1920 had developed into media events promoted and reported with due extravagance by press, radio and newsreels. The chief actors were the antagonists — Marty Welch, mild and gentlemanly; Clayt Morrissey, impatient and short-tempered; Piney, easygoing and humorous; and the villain or the champ, according to which side of the border claimed your allegiance, cagey old Angus, as most of those who sailed with him seemed to agree and Howard Chapelle wrote, "an aggressive, unsportsmanlike and abusive man, but a prime sailor."

As for the dirty tricks — the surreptitious shifting of the ballast, the disingenuous fouls, the conveniently unnoticed mark buoys, the midnight switching of the suits of sails and a few others that never came to light — such tomfoolery was not that uncharacteristic of the fishermen for whom a

214

practical joke was the finest kind, and yachtsmen's etiquette pure baloney.

The races did nothing to rationalize commercial fishing under sail in energy-abundant times, nor did they in any substantive way advance schooner design which, as Chapelle concluded, had reached its final evolution in smart vessels such as *Elsie*, mainly at the hands of McManus, Burgess and Lawlor back around the turn of the century and before. Helmsmen were not really all that different, other factors being fairly equal, and a good bigger boat, as they say, will generally beat a good smaller boat. Only the disqualified *Mayflower* was bigger than the *Bluenose*.

What should be cheerfully conceded from the Yankee point of view is that Jacobs, Welch, Morrissey, Thomas, Pine and so many of the other masters in the Gloucester fleet were in truth Canadians from the Maritime Provinces and Newfoundland. And *Bluenose* did so much for the pride of Canada up there under the shadow of Big Brother that a grateful people stamped her image permanently on their dime — truly a payback, in the coin of the Commonwealth, for eighty-six infinitely frustrating years of American possession of the Queen's Hundred Guineas Cup.

Great theater, the international races, the more so when it blew and there were a couple of cameramen on board. Ah, then the full show, pull out the stops, the wild skipper with everything flying, ready to carry away both sticks rather than be branded as a coward, the unflinching crews with teeth set and hands clenched, watching to see if their craft would stagger up again.

So fearless and ardent are the fishermen [observed Joseph Collins back before anyone thought of a formal race] that the better judgment of the skipper is frequently overcome by the solicitations of the crew, and in the hope of outstripping some rival vessel sail is carried in unreasonable excess. This is often the case when a vessel has just left port. The crew are then, perhaps, under the influence of spirituous liquors, which renders them more regardless of danger than common, and unable to properly perform their duty.

It is not uncommon for some of the more headstrong of the fishing skippers to carry so much sail on their vessels that the lee rail is completely under water most of the time. A few vessels may be able to stand being driven in this manner with comparative safety, but with the majority of them it is highly dangerous, and liable to result not only in the loss of the vessel by capsizing and filling, but also in the lives of the crew.

The races cost neither vessels nor lives. The truly hard old days were gone, and thank God for it, and Gloucester — by the twenties a long-established summer and artists' resort — was already coasting on its reputation as one of the world's saltiest ports. The playing-out of the international rivalry invested the ever-unappreciated fishermen of both countries, and in a sense their own special vessels, with a false glamour.

So much for the racing of fishing schooners. In the end they were a photographer's fantasy come true. Finally, as the last of the Gloucestermen, larger than life, played at the real thing, clinging like the Gloucestermen who sailed them to the semblance of times gone by, that mysterious, charismatic animation of these magical schooners was captured by the eye of the camera as never before.

Image had become reality.

WAKE

The schooners of Gloucester evolved and were conceived and born, tested, trained and worked. They played, idled and hibernated. They were vessels for all seasons. They triumphed, were wrecked, run down and drowned. They killed and rescued. They fell off into neglect and old age and died.

The spirit of the schooners was kindled by men. Their life was aroused by the sea and the wind, and ended by them. They were of wood, metal, hemp and cotton, and sailed by flesh and blood, and it is idolatry, after all, to endow them with creature qualities. Gloucestermen they were called, such steeds of the sea they seemed to be. But the true Gloucestermen were the men and not their steeds.

The Gloucester schooners are gone, all but four, all Essex-built. The *Lettie G. Howard* (A. D. Story in 1893) has been restored and sails with passengers out of New York's South Street Seaport. The big clipper-bowed *Ernestina*, ex-*Effie M. Morrissey* (Willard Burnham in 1894, ex-dory schooner, ex-Arctic explorer under Captain Bob Bartlett, ex-Cape Verde packet given by the islanders to the U.S. and likewise restored), sails out of New Bedford, likewise with passengers. The knockabout *L. A. Dunton* (A. D. Story in 1921) is a dockside museum at Mystic Seaport in Connecticut.

And the knockabout *Adventure* (James in 1926), the very last of the dory fishermen, is under restoration by her non-profit owner, The Gloucester Adventure, as a passenger-carrying educational vessel, a National Historic landmark, home at last.

All gone but four. But the men keep coming, through thick and thin, wind and wet — the Gloucestermen — still doing business in great waters.

ACKNOWLEDGEMENTS

At the heart of the Thomas Collection, and of *Down to the Sea,* are the glass plate negatives of Ernest L. Blatchford, manager of the New England Fish Company, a very superior amateur photographer with a journalistic eye, rare in his day, for both documentation and action. Almost as arresting but more serenely composed are those of a pioneer woman behind the lens, Martha Hale Harvey, wife of the Gloucester artist George W. Harvey; her scattered plates have been gathered from several sources. Of the other leading photographers represented in the Thomas Collection, Chester N. Walen had a particularly strong sense of the waterfront he grew up around; Robert W. Phelps, a local professional, and Herman W. Spooner (relatively few of whose superlative shots have survived) with Blatchford were members of the turn-of-the-century Cape Ann Camera Club, which stimulated much good recording of the scene that was so swiftly passing.

Aside from the photographic estates such as Blatchford's that he acquired, Thomas's *omnium-gatherum* reflects his fortunate compulsion to put his hands on at least one view of every Gloucester schooner caught by a camera from about the 1890s on, if it lay within begging, borrowing and frequently buying reach. For the purposes of *Down to the Sea* I wanted to round out the picture with more photographs from earlier in the last century, with a greater range taken at sea and with more shots of schooner construction. There are precious few examples in the first two categories because, I suspect, fishing under sail as a way of life was so taken for granted in the days before George Eastman revolutionized the camera that professional photographers rarely bothered to record it, and then almost invariably from shore, since their bulky equipment was hardly designed for a rolling deck. Even after it became the national fad, the Kodak was almost never taken on board by the fishermen, who had better things to do than to document the details of their daily drudgery.

At the Smithsonian Institution in Washington and The Mariners' Museum at Newport News, Virginia, I found small caches of vintage plates taken by T.W. Smillie in the early 1880s for the Goode Report. The Whaling

Museum at New Bedford opened up its collection of the surviving plates whereon Albert Cook Church recorded brilliantly not only the last of the whaling but the mackerel seiners and racing fishermen of Gloucester. The Peabody Museum of Salem made its famous archives as freely available. Dana Story's unequalled record of the Essex shipbuilding was the source of several gems, and he reviewed the building and racing chapters as well. More gaps were filled from the important collection of the affable Al Barnes at The Mariners' Museum, from the Cape Ann Historical Association's bulging packets of negatives exposed by the first-rate Gloucester amateur Eben Parsons and from its odds and ends, from my collection by Adolph Kupsincl, Chester M. Morrissey and others, and from the albums and files of numerous generous individuals.

Others who gave me friendly assistance with the pictorial side of this work include Elton W. Hall, Curator of Collections at the Whaling Museum, and Nick Whitman, Photo Editor; Paul B. Hensley, Archivist at The Mariners' Museum; Robert C. Post, Curator of the Section of Maritime History, National Museum of American History, Smithsonian Institution; Martin Horgan; Walter McNaney; and Jane Shannon Keniston.

I am indebted to Harry Eustis, Albert Johnson, William S. Webber, Jr., Douglas Parker, Richard V. Hunt, Paul B. Kenyon and Captains Morton Selig, Charles William Sibley and Thomas C. Morse, all of Gloucester; to Captain Leo Hynes of Nashua, New Hampshire, Charlie Sayle of Nantucket, and most particularly to Sterling Hayden, the one-time mastheadman who carries a part of Gloucester with him everywhere, and to the late Captain Lem Firth, Larry McEwen, Everett Jodrey, Charlie Olsen, Al Flygare, Jim Brennan, Charlie McPhee and Jim Walen, among so many others of Gloucester no longer with us — to all these and more for the *feel* of it. George O. Byard, whose heart is ever on the water, allowed me the run of the log of his grandfather, Eben Macauley. William P. Quinn of Orleans, down on Cape Cod, and Estella Hinckley of Gloucester supplied information on wrecks and the towboats of Cap Heberle. Warren F. Rathjen of the National Marine Fisheries Service at Gloucester produced helpful documents. The Sawyer Free Library of Gloucester was an essential resource as always.

My special appreciation goes to Harold Bell, president of the Cape Ann Historical Association, for providing me with the opportunity to take on a project so close to my core, and to Deborah L. Goodwin, curator, and Martha Oaks, assistant curator, for their competent assistance; to Gordon W. Thomas and his son Jeff, whose dedication to their family heritage, and to Gloucester's, has added a unique dimension to my efforts; to David R. Godine for the magic of his enthusiasm; to Deanne Smeltzer, my editor, for the magic of hers; to Gerry Morse, for her creative copyediting; to Richard C. Bartlett, whose inspired design has turned this into a work of art; and to H.B.G., whose light and loving touch is everywhere throughout.

J.E.G.

ACKNOWLEDGEMENTS

BIBLIOGRAPHY

Atlas of Essex County, Massachusetts. Philadelphia: D.G. Beers, 1872.

Babson, John J. *History of the Town of Gloucester* (1860). Reprinted, with introduction and historical update by Joseph E. Garland. Gloucester, Mass.: Peter Smith, Publisher, 1972.

Baker, William A. *Colonial Vessels.* Barre, Mass.: Barre Press, 1962.

Brooks, Alfred M. *Gloucester Recollected.* Gloucester, Mass.: Peter Smith, Publisher, 1974.

Chapelle, Howard I. *The American Fishing Schooners: 1825–1935.* New York: W.W. Norton & Co., Inc., 1973.

———. *The National Watercraft Collection.* U.S. National Museum Bulletin 219. Washington, 1960.

Cheney, Robert K. *Maritime History of the Merrimac.* Newburyport, Mass.: Newburyport Press, 1964.

Church, Albert C. "The Evolution and Development of the American Fishing Schooner." *Yachting,* May and June 1910.

Church, Albert C., and James B. Connolly. *American Fishermen.* New York: W. W. Norton & Co., Inc., 1940.

Collins, Joseph W. "Voyage of schooner *Marion,* 1879." In Goode's *Fisheries* V, 74 ff.

———. "Evolutions of the Fishing Schooner" (under "Management of the Vessels"). In Goode's *Fisheries* III, 130 ff.

Connolly, James B. *The Book of the Gloucester Fishermen.* New York: John Day Co., 1927.

Day, Thomas F. "The Schooner." *The Rudder,* March 1906.

Edson, Merritt A. "The Schooner Rig, A Hypothesis." *American Neptune,* April 1965.

Eliot, T. S. *Four Quartets.* New York: Harcourt Brace Jovanovich, Inc., 1943.

The Fisheries of Gloucester. Attributed to John J. Babson. Gloucester, Mass.: Procter Brothers, 1876.

Garland, J. Everett. *Journal of 1870s.* Author's collection.

Garland, Joseph E. "An ya don' know ware yer at?" (Joseph Mesquita). *Gloucester Daily Times,* March 29, 1968.

———. "A Bank Trip in the 90s" (Eben Macauley). *Ibid.,* December 4, 6, and 8, 1967.

———. "The Brennan Tapes" (James E. Brennan). *North Shore '74,* February 9, 1974.

———. "A Cloud of Sorrow" (gale of February 1879). *Gloucester Magazine,* fall 1979.

———. *Lone Voyager* (1963). Reprinted, Rockport, Mass.:N. B. Robinson, 1978.

Gillespie, G. J. *Bluenose Skipper.* Fredericton, New Brunswick: Brunswick Press, 1955.

Goode, G. Browne, et al. *The Fisheries and Fishery Industries of the United States,* 6 vols. Washington: U.S. Commission of Fish & Fisheries, 1887.

Hayden, Sterling. *Wanderer.* New York: Alfred A. Knopf, Inc., 1963.

Herreshoff, L. Francis. *The Common Sense of Yacht Design.* Jamaica, N.Y.: Caravan-Maritime Books, 1966.

Hill, Walter. "A Winter's Trip to Georges." In Procter, *The Fisherman's Own Book. Ibid.*

History of Essex County, Massachusetts. Ed. D. Hamilton Hurd. 2 vols. Philadelphia: J. W. Lewis, 1888.

Innis, Harold A. *The Cod Fisheries*. Toronto: University of Toronto Press, 1954.

Kipling, Rudyard. *Captains Courageous*. New York: Century Printing Co., 1896.

Madsen, Betsy R., and Burnham, Maria. *Dubbing, Hooping, and Lofting: Shipbuilding Skills*. Essex, Mass.: Essex Shipbuilding Museum, 1981.

McFarland, Raymond. *The Masts of Gloucester*. New York: W. W. Norton & Co., 1937.

McLaren, R. Keith. *Bluenose and Bluenose II*. Willowdale, Ontario: Hounslow Press, 1981.

Memorial of the Celebration of the 250th Anniversary of the Incorporation of the Town of Gloucester, Mass., August 1892. Boston: City of Gloucester, 1901.

Mills, Ruth W. *George Marble Wonson: His Forebears and Descendants*. Gloucester, Mass., 1958.

Morison, Samuel E. *The Maritime History of Massachusetts 1783-1860*. Boston: Houghton Mifflin Co., 1921.

Morris, E. P. *The Fore-and-Aft Rig in America*. New Haven: Yale University Press, 1927.

O'Hearn, Joseph C. *New England Fishing Schooners*. Milwaukee: Kalmbach Publishing Co., 1947.

Paintings and Drawings by Fitz Hugh Lane at the Cape Ann Historical Association. Gloucester, Mass., 1974.

Phelps, Elizabeth S. "The Stone Woman of Eastern Point." In *Memorial of the 250th Anniversary*, pp. 336-337.

———. *Chapters from a Life*. Boston: Houghton Mifflin Co., 1896.

Pierce, Wesley G. *Goin' Fishin'*. Salem, Mass.: Marine Research Society, 1934.

Procter, George H. *The Fishermen's Memorial and Record Book*. Gloucester, Mass.: Procter Brothers, 1873.

———. *The Fishermen's Own Book*. Gloucester, Mass.: Procter Brothers, 1882.

Robinson, Bill. *The World of Yachting*. New York: Random House, Inc., 1966.

Ship Registers of the District of Gloucester Massachusetts 1789-1875. Salem, Mass.: The Essex Institute, 1944.

Smith, Sylvanus. *Fisheries of Cape Ann*. Gloucester, Mass.: The Gloucester Times, 1915.

Stanford, Alfred. *Men, Fish and Boats*. Jersey City, N.J.: William Morrow & Co., Inc., 1934.

Story, Dana A. *An Approximate Listing of the Vessels, Boats and Other Craft Built in the Town of Essex, 1870 through 1977. Based upon the Research and Listings of Lewis H. Story, Essex*. Essex, Mass. (photocopied), 1978.

———. *Frame-Up!* Barre, Mass.: Barre Press, 1964.

———. *Hail Columbia!* Barre, Mass.: Barre Press, 1970.

Story, Dana A., and John M. Clayton. *The Building of a Wooden Ship*. Barre, Mass.: Barre Press, 1971.

Thomas, Gordon W. *Fast and Able*. Gloucester, Mass.: Gloucester 350th Anniversary Celebration, Inc., 1973.

———. *Wharf and Fleet*. Gloucester, Mass.: Nautical Reproductions of Gloucester, 1977.

Wallace, Frederick W. "Life on the Grand Banks." *National Geographic Magazine*, July 1921.

Wallen, Frederick M. "Life on Board a Fishing Schooner at Sea." In *Report of the Commissioner for 1878*. United States Commission of Fish and Fisheries, Washington, 1880.

Webber, William S., Jr. *Waterfront*. Gloucester, Mass.: Cape Ann Savings Bank, 1973.

NEWSPAPERS

Cape Ann Weekly Advertiser, Gloucester Telegraph, Gloucester Daily Times

INDEX

DOWN TO THE SEA

INDEX

Down to the Sea

is set in Meridien, a Mergenthaler VIP font strongly influenced by Eric Gill's Monotype design Perpetua. It has a sturdiness, grace and utility that makes it right for a book on the fishing schooners of Gloucester.

Designed by Richard C. Bartlett, the book was set by Lujean Printing Company, Inc., Santuit, Massachusetts. *Down to the Sea* was printed on acid-free paper by Norman Graphic Printing Company, Hong Kong.

Maps by Jacqueline Sakwa. Decorative line drawings by Richard F. Bartlett.

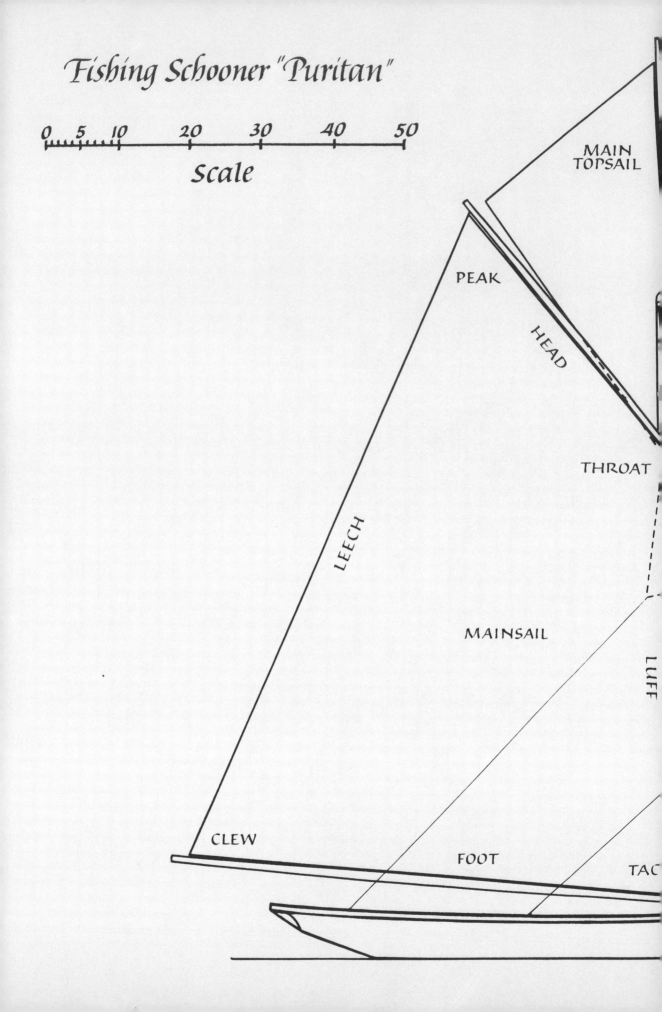

Fishing Schooner "Puritan"

Scale

0 5 10   20   30   40   50

MAIN
TOPSAIL

PEAK

HEAD

THROAT

LEECH

MAINSAIL

LUFF

CLEW

FOOT

TAC

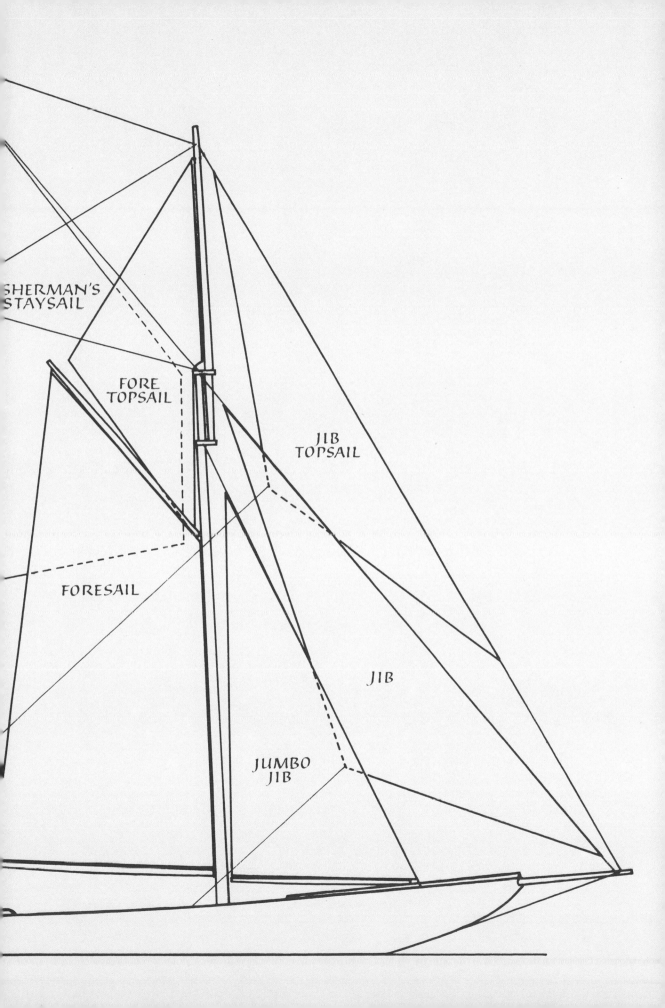